WARGAMING WORLD WAR TWO

WARGAMING WORLD WAR TWO

Stuart Asquith

ARGUS BOOKS

Argus Books
Argus House
Boundary Way
Hemel Hempstead
Herts. HP2 7ST
England

First published by Argus Books 1989

Phototypesetting by Gilbert Composing Services, Leighton Buzzard
Printed and bound in Great Britain by Richard Clay Ltd, Bungay, Suffolk

CONTENTS

ACKNOWLEDGEMENTS

I would like to thank the many people who have helped in the production of this book, among them Gordon Brown of Cromwell Models, Steve Cox of Skytrex, Simon Hoare of The Harrow Model Shop, Bob Johnsey of Quartermasters Stores, Cameron Robinson of Model Figures and Hobbies, Terry Wise of Athena Books, Alan Woods and Steve Woods. Particular thanks are also due to Ken Jones, editor of "Military Modelling" and to Folly Marland and Rab MacWilliam of Argus Books for all their technical assistance and support throughout the project. Finally, thanks to Daisy for making the original manuscript so presentable.

Introduction

Some periods in wargaming continue to enjoy a sizeable following, while others seem to enjoy only a fleeting spell in the limelight. World War Two has consistently proved to be an extremely popular wargames period with countless numbers of adherents. Why this should be the case is difficult to determine, but the fact remains that there is an absolute wealth of model aeroplanes, armoured fighting vehicles and figures available.

World War Two encompasses virtually all nations and every conceivable type of terrain, as well as combat in the air and at sea, so the wargamer is never at a loss for a situation to re-fight. Many types of game—small raiding parties, partisan warfare, large battles, air raids, fleet actions, coastal assaults and armoured conflicts—are all quite possible within the parameters of the conflict.

The idea behind this particular book is to write not just another history book on World War Two, but to look at the differing nature of the combat on land, at sea and in the air, and to reflect this in some suggested rules for the wargamer to use when recreating such actions. The overall aims are to interest and inspire those wargamers who do not play the period and to offer fresh ideas and rule mechanisms for those who already do.

Following a year-by-year review of the war, the book is divided into three main sections—land, sea and air combat. A degree of factual and historical background is necessary, both for placing battles in their correct historical perspective and for examining the capabilities of the various aircraft, vehicles and weapons which were involved. These sections cover the organisations of the main combatant countries, look at the equipment that was used, offer some wargame rules and then suggest some scenarios which can be played out on the table top. An indication as to the availability and range of kits, models and figures is included, along with a selection of relevant and interesting titles for further reading. Although each section is fairly self-contained, there is a degree of overlap between them, which serves perhaps to underline the co-operation necessary between the varying arms of the services.

This is a book which I enjoyed writing and I hope that this enthusiasm conveys itself within the text. If the reader enjoys the book and feels inspired as a result, then the book will have achieved its purpose.

1 General Analysis of the War

Although by far the greater part of this book will be concerned with wargaming, a certain amount of historical perspective is essential, in order that the reader can more readily appreciate the background against which the various rules have been formulated. Furthermore, if the wargamer is not entirely happy with a particular rule mechanism, or a suggested interpretation does not sit well with him, then he is able to assimilate the context in which it was formed for himself and perhaps draw his own conclusions.

I propose to examine World War Two year by year, rather than follow through a particular campaign in its entirety which would necessitate covering a number of years. The main reason for doing this is that the wargamer usually has armies based on their historical counterparts at a given date in the War. Seldom does the table top general organise an army specifically for the Allied advance on Rome for example, but one can frequently see miniature formations based on the British and American forces of, say, 1944. While only the major actions and campaigns can be covered, it is interesting both to see the general outline of what was taking place during each year of the War and to examine the potential for one's miniature armies.

Naturally, it will still be possible to trace the course of a particular campaign as the events of each year are analysed and summarised. One aspect which will be unique to this particular chapter is that the land, sea and air battles will be considered as being inter-connected, inter-related and inter-dependent parts of the conflict. In later chapters of the book, the three will be treated as separate entities for ease of reference by the reader.

1939

The Polish Campaign

The 1st of September 1939 marked the start of World War Two, as over a million German troops invaded Poland from the north, south and west in the start of the short Polish Campaign, codenamed

Weiss Fall. The nine armoured and 51 infantry divisions organised into two Army Groups under Marshal von Brauchitsch struck through the six Polish armies as though they did not exist. From the north came General Fedor von Bock's Group consisting of the Third and Fourth Armies, whilst the Eighth, Tenth and Fourteenth Armies under General Gerd von Rundstedt swept basically eastwards.

No formal declaration of war had been made prior to the invasion and the German invasion, coupled as it was with close artillery air support, overwhelmed the Polish forces. Much of the Polish Air Force was destroyed on the ground and the tiny navy was easily neutralised in the Gulf of Danzig. The Polish army was outclassed and outnumbered in all aspects by the Germans. It is in this campaign—largely during the battle of Warsaw—that one reads of the myth of Polish cavalry charging German tanks. In point of fact, the campaign was not that easy for the Germans, as the Poles, although outnumbered, offered a spirited resistance. Indeed, the Polish army had little else to offer in the way of defence against the onslaught thrown at them. Working to a well-prepared plan, the Germans made good use of sympathisers in the Polish population and always had the benefit of first class intelligence regarding Polish dispositions.

"Blitzkreig", meaning 'lightning war', had begun and a startling demonstration of its devastating efficiency had been given to all who cared to take notice. Earlier in 1939, Adolf Hitler, the German leader, had negotiated a secret non-aggression pact with Russia. This document was signed just seven days before the orders to cross Poland's borders were put into action. Russia was seen as a neutral power but, about a fortnight after the German invasion, Russian troops crossed Poland's eastern border and totally swamped any resistance. Poland surrendered on October 5th.

Western Europe

As a result of the invasion of Poland, France and Great Britain declared war on Germany on September 3rd. This declaration was followed by a period of inactivity, often referred to as the 'phony war' reflecting the lack of any meaningful activity. Mobilisation was under way, certainly, but there was no aggression being offered at this stage. France had faith in her Maginot Line—a long line of concrete and steel fortresses on her eastern border—and Belgium and Holland declared their neutrality. Thus, the Allied powers did nothing to counter the very action which had brought them into the War, leaving Germany to operate unhindered in Eastern Europe. Great Britain shipped an Expeditionary Force across the English Channel, in much the same manner as in 1914. These troops were concentrated in France, but remained immobile at a time when a decisive move westwards could have stopped the German operations. Alas, hindsight is the weapon of the armchair general and the Allied commanders settled for a policy of static defence and an economic blockade of Germany.

The Finnish–Russian War

Following her involvement in the Polish campaign, Russia sought the support of her near neighbours, Estonia, Latvia and Lithuania. In return Russia sent troops to those countries to "assist with their defence". Finland, however, would have none of it, rejected all Russian proposals and mobilised her armies. The Russian response was swift and overpowering, with almost a million troops invading Finland in late November, eventually swamping all Finnish resistance. Not that this was a repeat of the Polish experience—the Finns were well led by their commander von Mannerheim and the Russian attacks were more often than not muddled affairs with little or no co-ordination. It is true to say that it was the overwhelming Russian numbers that won the day, rather than any military skill. A blitzkreig this was not. Finland finally surrendered on March 12th 1940, but her gallant stand had exposed the Russians as blundering and unscientific, a fact Hitler was to note carefully.

Events at Sea

It is true to say that the naval war opened with the sinking on September 3rd of the British passenger liner *Athenia* by a German submarine, or 'U-boat' as they were termed. Two weeks later the aircraft carrier HMS *Courageous* was sunk, also by a U-boat, as was the battleship HMS *Royal Oak*. Under the terms of the Versailles Treaty, drawn up at the end of World War One, Germany was forbidden to build ships of over 10,000 tons. In order to circumvent these restrictions the German navy started to build vessels which were known as *panzerschiff* or "pocket battleships". These ships were in reality battle cruisers carrying heavy calibre guns but which, in order to comply with the legislation, did not have very much armour. Hence they were well-armed and fast, but lacked the defensive protection of a full battleship.

In September one of these vessels, the *Admiral Graf Spee*, embarked on a cruise of destruction in the Indian Ocean and the South Atlantic. Before she was finally engaged in the Battle of the River Plate in December by HMS *Achilles, Ajax* and *Exeter*, and trapped and forced to scuttle, the *Graf Spee* sank many tons of Allied shipping. German naval headquarters was well aware of the shortcomings of their pocket battleships. They would not stand much of a chance in a straight fight with the more numerous and heavier capital ships of the Royal Navy but, as commerce raiders, powerful and with a sufficient turn of speed to act either alone or in small numbers, they were deadly. Other vessels, such as the prototype pocket battleship *Deutschland* (later re-named *Lutzow*) and the battle cruisers *Gneisenau* and *Scharnhorst*, carried out numerous missions against Allied shipping in the Atlantic in an attempt to disrupt the Allies' supply lines.

1940

The Invasion of Norway

Hitler's next move was to invade Denmark and Norway in Operation *Weserubung*. Swedish iron ore, an important factor in German industrial strength, was imported either through the Baltic Sea or along the Norwegian coastline. The Royal Navy, following Britain's blockading policy against Germany, was a constant threat to the latter and most important route, but its ships were beyond the range of aircraft based within Germany. By securing forward bases in Norway, the German air force, or Luftwaffe, would be able to add their weight to the attack on the blockading vessels. Looking further ahead, these same airfields would also form a useful base for the planned assault on England.

Early April saw a number of minor naval actions along the Norwegian coast, as units of the Royal Navy tried unsuccessfully to prevent some of the German troop convoys from reaching their destinations. In early April, German units crossed the border into Denmark, which fell quickly with little or no bloodshed. At the same time, the efficiently conducted German invasion of Norway was under way and while more opposition was encountered, that country also came under German domination. Allied troops— originally intended to assist Finland's struggle but unable to do so due to lack of time—were landed to support the Norwegian army. The German reaction was swift and there were fierce battles for the key towns, among them Narvik and Trondheim. Eventually, due to events in France which we shall look at later, the Allied troops were evacuated from Narvik in early June. In the course of the evacuation, the aircraft carrier HMS *Glorious* was sunk, but, in turn, the German battle cruisers *Gneisenau* and *Scharnhorst* were sufficiently damaged to render them inoperable for months.

The Fall of France

By May 1940, three German Army Groups were assembled along her western borders from Holland to Switzerland in accordance with the Manstein Plan, laid out for just such an event. Army Group A, destined for the Ardennes, was led by General von Runstedt and had four armies (Busch's 16th, Kluge's 4th, List's 12th, Strauss' 9th and

Weich's 2nd) supported by an armoured group under Kleist which contained most of the tanks allotted to the force. Army Group B which, it was planned, would over-run Holland, was under the command of von Bock and consisted of two armies (Kuechler's 18th and Reichenau's 6th), while von Leeb's Army Group C, initially performing a supportive function, was of a similar size (Dollman's 7th and Witzleben's 1st). This massive land force—about two and a half million soldiers—was supported by 3,500 aircraft and was under the direct command of Adolf Hitler himself.

Arrayed against this might, the Allies had three Army Groups which consisted for the most part of French troops. The First Group which included the British Expeditionary Force under Lord Gort had four other armies (Blanchard's 1st, Corap's 9th, Giraud's 7th and Huntzinger's 2nd) led by General Billotte. The Second Group of three armies (Bourret's 5th, Conde's 3rd and Requin's 4th) was under the command of General Pretelat, whilst General Besson had the single army (Garchery's 8th) which made up the Third Group. The Allied commander-in-chief was General Gamelin, while General Georges exercised field command over virtually two million men. Still more Allied soldiers manned the Maginot Line defences and the French Air Force mustered 1,400 planes, the Royal Air Force just under 300. Sheltering under their fragile umbrella of supposed neutrality, the Dutch army consisted of 400,000 poorly equipped and badly trained men, while the Belgians had 600,000 troops in a similar condition. Both countries, however, possessed good natural defences, formed by extensive canals and the potential for flooding huge areas of land.

Dunkirk

On May 10th 1940 the blow fell and the 'Phony War' came well and truly to an end. With a repeat of the Blitzkreig tactics so successfully tested in Poland, this time with the additional support provided by advance drops of paratroops, the German armies moved into the neutral Netherlands. By May 14th Holland had fallen; a day later, Belgium. While the Low Countries were under attack, Army Group A moved through the Ardennes, capitalised on a gap created by the shattered French 9th Army and drove on for the Channel coast. The continuing German pressure forced the Allied units ever westwards into a continually tightening defensive position.

The end of May saw the Belgian surrender, which had the effect of exposing the Allied left flank, and an evacuation of British troops from the only port in Allied hands, Dunkirk, was speedily put into action as Operation *Dynamo*. For some reason, Hitler ordered his armies to halt just as they were closing in on the beleaguered British Expeditionary Force and their Belgian and French allies.

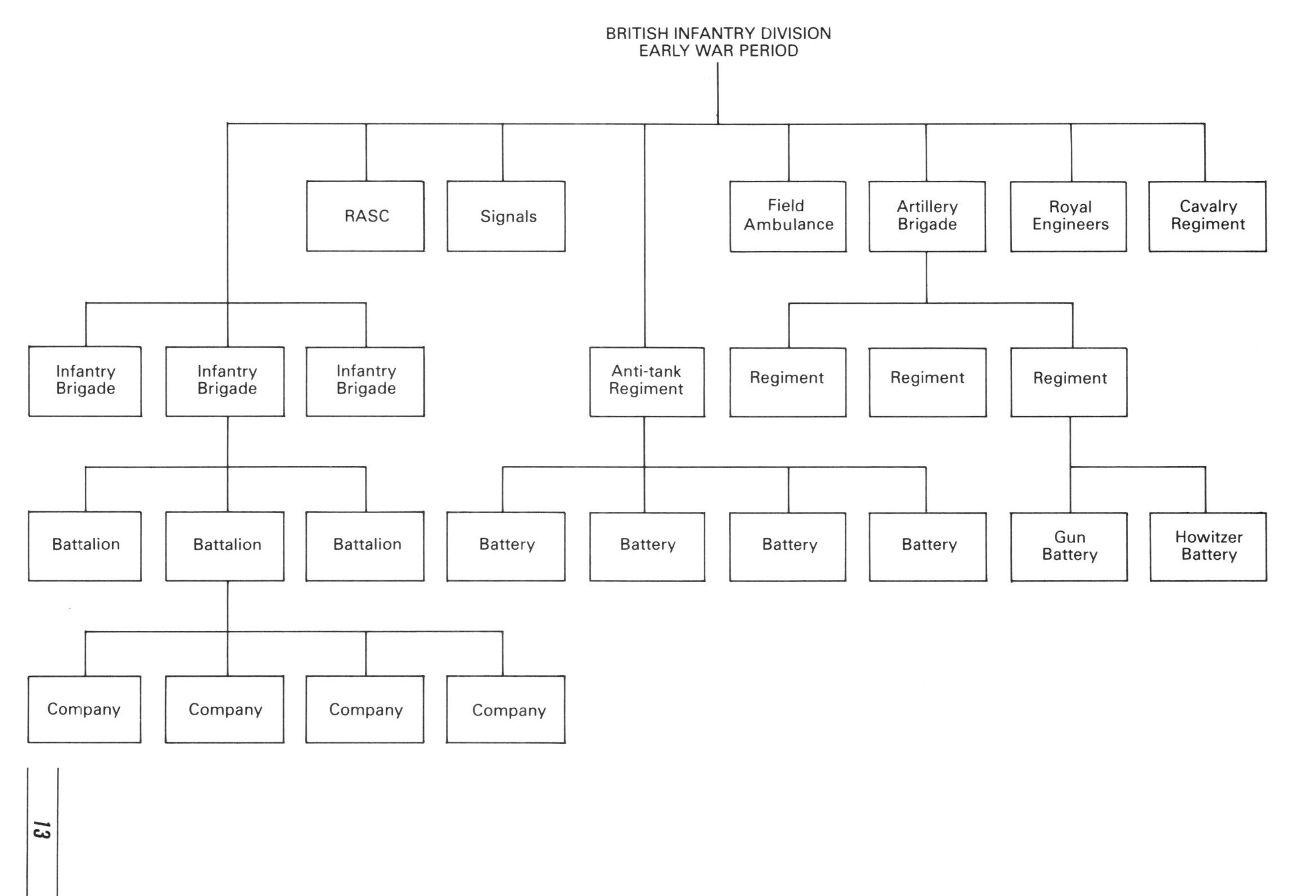

BRITISH INFANTRY DIVISION
EARLY WAR PERIOD
RASC
Signals
Field Ambulance
Artillery Brigade
Royal Engineers
Cavalry Regiment
Infantry Brigade
Infantry Brigade
Infantry Brigade
Anti-tank Regiment
Regiment
Regiment
Regiment
Battalion
Battalion
Battalion
Battery
Battery
Battery
Battery
Gun Battery
Howitzer Battery
Company
Company
Company
Company

There are many theories as to why this amazing order was issued, but no one will ever really know for sure. The consensus of opinion is that Hitler wanted his Luftwaffe to add the finishing touch to the campaign and destroy the Allied armies. Certainly this would have had the merit of saving German lives but, in the event, the efforts of the Luftwaffe were ably countered by the Royal Air Force. The Dunkirk evacuation, courageously carried out by ships of the Royal Navy, of commercial companies and of private individuals, was able to rescue nearly 340,000 British and Allied troops in just over a week, albeit without their equipment and weapons.

Italy enters the war

Following the evacuation, the battle of France continued throughout most of June. Driving remorselessly south and south-west, the German armies carved their way through the demoralised and understrength French forces. On June 10th, Italy, judging that France was lost, declared war on her and sent troops to invade the south of the country. Eleven days later France surrendered with more than half of her lands under German control. To all intents and purposes, Hitler was now the undisputed master of Western Europe.

The Battle of Britain

The fall of France meant that Britain stood alone against the German forces. This was not quite the case, however, for the British Empire was still very much intact in 1940, with Australia, Canada, India, New Zealand and South Africa mobilising themselves for war. Further, shipments of arms and ammunition which had been purchased began to arrive from the United States of America to start the re-equipping of the British Army. Brigadier General de Gaulle began to organise the Free French forces in Africa and the Middle East and the French Navy was either sunk to prevent it falling into German hands, as at Oran, or handed over to the Free French, as happened at Alexandria. Early in June, Hitler, against the advice of some of his senior commanders but with the full approval of the Luftwaffe, decided to invade England in Operation *Seelowe*.

For such an enterprise to succeed, control of the sea was a vital factor. As we have already seen, the German navy was considered no match for the Royal Navy, so the task was given to the Luftwaffe to be carried out in two distinct phases. Firstly the Royal Air Force was to be defeated and, once air superiority had been achieved, attention would be turned to the Royal Navy. The Luftwaffe, led by Air Marshal Goering, saw themselves as invincible, for thus far they had swept all before them—with the notable and significant exception of Dunkirk—and they now had the use of airfields in

France, the Low Countries and Norway, which greatly increased their operational ranges.

The Battle of Britain can be divided into a number of phases, which will be summarised below. Initially (August 8th to 18th), the Luftwaffe strategy was to engage the RAF fighters in aerial combat and to this end they used three air forces, one based in northern France, another in Belgium and Holland and a third operating from Norwegian bases. Britain was heavily outnumbered in terms of aircraft, but she did have the advantage of the newly developed radar, which enabled the RAF to plot the course of the Luftwaffe formations and to bring local superiority to bear on them. At the end of this first phase the sky over the British Isles still belonged to the RAF.

Frustrated by their lack of success, the focus of the Luftwaffe's attention shifted to the RAF's airfields. Between August 24th and September 5th, wave after wave of bombers attacked British bases, inflicting great damage both to the airfields themselves and to communications, making concerted response more difficult. There is little doubt that, if this phase had been allowed to continue, the RAF would have gone under and Goering's aim would have been achieved. During August, the RAF mounted a retaliatory air raid on the German capital, Berlin. This was followed by raids on several other German cities, where the actual damage caused was negligible, but the psychological effect was tremendous. An enraged Hitler called an end to the attacks on British airfields and instead ordered the concentration of reprisal bombing on London (September 7th to 30th) which was to form the next phase of the Battle of Britain.

Civilian casualties inevitably were high and the damage caused was considerable, but the Luftwaffe also lost many planes and men in the process. While this phase was in progress, the RAF and elements of the Royal Navy destroyed a great number of troop transport barges which the Germans had amassed in preparation for their invasion. This successful mission had the effect of making Hitler postpone his planned Operation *Seelowe*, causing the raids on London to diminish. While sporadic raids continued, October 1st to 30th can be seen as the final stage of the battle. Defeated partly by the British will to survive and partly by the continual German dissipation of effort, Hitler cancelled the invasion and turned his attention elsewhere. In November the bombing of the British Isles—'The Blitz'—and, in a more or less continuous period lasting until May 1941, almost 100,000 civilians were killed or wounded, with London and Coventry being particularly badly hit. In real terms, however, the Battle of Britain was over.

The Axis Powers

On September 27th an agreement was signed between Germany, Italy and Japan. Each country promised to help the other two for the next ten years, but the agreement did not at the time ask Japan to take up arms. The term 'Axis' was first used by the Italian leader Mussolini as a description of the common aims of Germany and Italy.

The Western Desert

The Mediterranean was a vital link in Britain's supply lines, as was the Suez Canal where her forces were deployed to retain its possession. In June, as well as preparing for operations against British Somaliland, Kenya and the Sudan, Mussolini planned to take the canal by force by attacking simultaneously from the south-east and the west. To coincide with this, an Italian move on Greece was planned. The British Prime Minister and war leader, Winston Churchill, recognised the threat posed by these moves and despatched Britain's only remaining armoured division to Egypt in June to bolster the defence of the Suez Canal. General Wavell was the British commander in the area and his troops were scattered throughout North Africa with only 36,000 in Egypt. He was also short of air power with which to face the Italian air force, and the Mediterranean Fleet would have to take on the full might of the Italian navy.

On September 13th the invasion of Egypt began as the Italians moved along the coastline, the light British forces falling back in front of them. The British counter-attack was held up, for Wavell was instructed to send men to occupy Crete and most of his aircraft to help the resistance of the Italian invasion of Greece, which had begun in late October. Their weight and firepower were instrumental in helping the Greek forces successfully repel the Italians. Finally, in early December, Wavell was able to assume the offensive and in Operation *Compass*, a daring eastwards assault which was supported both by the RAF and off-shore naval gunfire, threw the Italians completely out of Egypt.

Events at Sea

In exchange for the use of eight of her bases in and around the Americas, the United States gave Britain 50 elderly destroyers, for Britain did not have enough light escort vessels and her shipyards could not hope to meet the demand for them. The German pocket battleship *Admiral Scheer* escaped the blockading naval forces and attacked Allied shipping in the North Atlantic, South Atlantic and Indian oceans. The heavy cruiser *Hipper* also ventured out into the Atlantic, but it was the sea-going presence in May of the largest and most powerful warship of its time, the *Bismarck*, that caused the most concern to the Allies. In company with the heavy cruiser *Prinz Eugen*, the *Bismarck* was sought by all available Allied naval units. In one attempt to stop the German ships, HMS *Hood* was sunk and HMS *Prince of Wales* damaged. Doggedly pursued by the Royal Navy, the *Bismarck* was at last cornered by HMS *Ark Royal*, allowing the battleships HMS *King George V* and *Rodney* to close and engage her. On May 28th the *Bismarck* was sunk after the *Prinz Eugen* had managed to evade her pursuers.

It was not only the German surface raiders that were causing problems. Under the able leadership of Admiral Doenitz, the U-boats were also inflicting increasingly heavy losses on Allied shipping in the North Atlantic as the merchantmen carried their cargos from the United States to the British Isles. Hunting in groups—'wolfpacks' as they became known—the U-boats sank solitary ships with ease. To counter this the convoy system, by no means unique to World War Two, was re-introduced, whereby a varying number of merchant ships would sail as a group, protected by naval vessels. This was only partially successful for, when in sufficient strength, the U-boats took on even the largest convoys. As if this menace was not sufficient, the convoys were also vulnerable to German long-range bombers which now operated from bases in Western Europe. This airborne menace caused the convoy to gain its own air cover by virtue of the escort carrier, often just a merchant ship with a temporary flight deck added.

1941

Wavell's Offensives
General Wavell resumed the offensive and seized Tobruk from the Italians at the end of January. This was eventually followed by a total surrender of the Italian forces. In two months General Wavell had covered 500 miles and, aided by naval and air support, destroyed a much larger Italian army. Attention now turned to Italian East Africa, the 'back door' to the Western Desert, with Wavell moving against Ethiopia and Italian Somaliland as other thrusts were directed from the Sudan and Kenya.

By May, after a well-conducted, fast-moving campaign, Addis Ababa was taken, the Emperor Haile Selassie restored and the Italian presence snuffed out. So desperate was the Italian position that Hitler was forced to send General Rommel with his famed Afrika Korps to Tripolitania to take over Axis operations against Egypt and the Suez Canal. Rommel immediately counter-attacked, driving the Allies back westwards on Tobruk which at once became the target for some concerted German attacks. The siege of Tobruk became a focus of attention and the scene of some of the fiercest fighting of the entire war. In July, General Wavell was replaced by General Auchinleck and the renowned Eighth Army came into being as, towards the end of the year, yet another Allied offensive was launched. After numerous actions, Rommel was pushed back eastwards and the end of 1941 saw the Germans back in the positions that they had held at the start of the year. German-activated revolts in Iraq and Syria served to compound General Wavell's problems. Some of his troops were sent to deal with the situation, with Wavell himself leading a successful advance into Syria from Palestine.

The Balkans

In preparation for his intended invasion of Russia, Hitler had to secure what would be his southern flank by taking control of Yugoslavia. Sensing that this might happen, the British government despatched more of Wavell's men to Greece, where they landed in March. The Yugoslav government, which had been pressurised into subservience by Hitler, was overthrown and its replacement rejected any co-operation with the Germans. A rapidly planned German invasion ended with the unconditional surrender of the partially mobilised Yugoslav forces in April. Simultaneously with the Yugoslavian move, Operation *Marita* saw German troops successfully invading Greece. Following an efficient and precisely planned campaign, Greek resistance crumbled and the British forces were evacuated.

The Battle for Crete

In late April and early May, some of the British troops rescued from Greece were landed in Crete, which was seen as the Germans' next objective. These were joined by more men from Egypt and the island's own Greek garrison as they awaited the onslaught. Operating from bases in southern Greece, German airborne forces landed to seize the Cretan airfields—Operation *Merkur*, the first major airborne assault of the war, was underway. While suffering extremely heavy casualties, the German paratroopers managed to secure a sufficiently strong foothold to permit reinforcements to be flown in. Thus strengthened, the German forces advanced and, although some of the defenders were evacuated by sea, many were forced to surrender and were taken prisoner.

The Invasion of Russia

After a three week delay caused by the Balkans campaign, Operation *Barbarossa*, the German invasion of Russia, was launched on June 22nd. The immense size of the undertaking defies a mere summary. Around three million German troops were involved, with a similar number of Russians. In all, ten armies and four armoured groups took part in the invasion—Runstedt's Army Group South (three German armies, one Rumanian) and the 1st Panzer Group was to move against Kiev and the valley of the Dnieper; Bock's Army Group Centre (two armies) with the 2nd and 3rd Panzer Groups was to capture Moscow; and Leeb's Army Group North (two armies) and the 4th Panzer Group took Leningrad. A Finnish force also threatened that city, while troops from Norway cut Russian supply lines.

The Russians, for their part, deployed in a largely linear defence, their left or southern flank on the Black Sea, their right on the northern Finnish coast. As the Germans advanced on a 2,000 mile front, Minsk and Smolensk were swiftly taken by Bock's Group which moved more quickly than its flanking formations. Concerned at the relatively slow progress of the Northern and Southern Groups, Hitler re-adjusted their composition, a move which resulted in the taking of Kiev and the trapping of five Russian armies in a loop of the Dneiper River. However, there were other, further reaching effects of these changes. By October and November, the German commanders had accomplished an amazing feat of arms, but their supply lines were becoming longer and the now slower-moving nature of the conflict was taking its toll on the machinery of war.

Hitler had viewed *Barbarossa* as a four month operation and no allowances had been made for a winter campaign. Although the Germans were still winning all their battles, they were losing out to time. By the end of 1941 Russian resistance had become more stable, bolstered by a seemingly endless supply of fresh, dedicated, if untried, troops from the east of the country. The defence of Moscow was seen as both the physical and symbolic centre of a determined Russian resistance against the German invader. German troops came to within twenty-five miles of the city, but their offensive ground to a halt in the face of a severe Russian winter for which they were totally unprepared. Early December witnessed the first Russian counters and, by the turn of the year, German forces were giving ground.

America Enters the Conflict
While the United States had been supplying help to the Allies, she was still not officially at war. In October of 1941 Japan laid down a three-point plan for the defeat of the Allies, and the first phase of this called for the elimination, or at least the neutralisation, of the US Pacific Fleet. The fleet, which was the main opposition to the Japanese in the Pacific, was based at Pearl Harbor in Hawaii. In a surprise air strike directed against Pearl Harbor, the Japanese

achieved their aim and put the US fleet out of action for nearly a year. The attack changed the state of affairs overnight and on the following day, December 8th, the United States declared war. Three days later Germany and Italy returned the compliment and America mobilised.

Japanese Moves

At the same time as the attack on Pearl Harbor, Japanese land forces were also on the move. The US possessions of Guam and Wake Island in the central Pacific were taken, as was the British territory of Hong Kong. The Malayan peninsula was invaded and the end of the year saw the British defenders being pushed remorselessly towards Singapore, situated on the very tip of the country. The Philippines, lying to the south of Japan, were also attacked with the capital, Manila, being declared an open city and the islands of Luzon, Mindanao and Jolo being captured.

Events at Sea

In the Mediterranean, German air power disrupted Allied naval operations and the important base of Malta was under constant attack. In March, the Italian navy set sail to harass the progress of British reinforcements despatched to Greece from Egypt. Admiral Cunningham sent the troopships back to port and set out to engage the Italians. At the resulting battle of Cape Matapan (March 28th), Cunningham mauled them to such a degree that they were never again a force to be considered for the rest of the war. Operating in support of the numerous land-based operations taking place on the Mediterranean coastline, Cunningham's force suffered severe losses—the aircraft carrier HMS *Ark Royal* and the battleship HMS *Barham* were sunk, and the battleships HMS *Queen Elizabeth* and HMS *Valiant* were badly damaged. Seeking to engage the Japanese vessels which were supporting the invasion of Malaya, the battleship HMS *Prince of Wales* and the battlecruiser HMS *Repulse* were sunk by Japanese aircraft.

Moving to somewhat colder climes, British convoys were started in August to supply Russia in her stand against Hitler. The run to the port of Murmansk was a dangerous undertaking, the ships involved being at risk from both the Germans and the severe weather, but the convoys continued to provide much needed aid to Russia.

1942

Coastal Raids

In March, an Allied mission was sent to knock out the dry dock at St. Nazaire. This was the only one of a sufficient size, outside Germany, that was capable of holding the battleship *Tirpitz*, which was identical in size to the *Bismarck*. The raid featured the use of an old destroyer packed with explosives and was extremely successful, rendering the dock unusable. In August, a much larger raid against Dieppe was carried out by British and Canadian units. Although the raid itself was a failure, the exercise provided some vital lessons which were to be of immense value in later amphibious operations.

North Africa

Auchinleck and Rommel faced one another in Cyrenaica but, by the end of January, the Germans had once again assumed the offensive. The battle of Gazala in late May/early June was followed by the loss of Tobruk and by a British retreat into Egypt in the face of a bold German advance. General Montgomery took over command of the Eighth Army and halted Rommel at the battle of Alam Halfa in September. After spending the better part of two months in preparation, Montgomery defeated the Germans in the decisive battle of El Alamein at the end of October. Allied morale was heartened and pursuing units continually harrassed Rommel's retreat, defeating him in a number of actions such as Mersa Matruh.

While this pursuit was taking place, Allied troops were landing in Algeria and Morocco under Operation *Torch* to establish bases for further operations. The operation was the largest amphibious exercise of the war so far, with three Task Forces—Western (General Patton 35,000 men) which was aimed at Casablanca, Central (General Frenedall 39,000) intended to seize Oran and Eastern (General Ryder 33,000) which would concentrate on Algiers. All the Task Forces had naval support and all were under the supreme command of General Eisenhower. Some units of the Vichy (German collaborating) French army and navy offered some resistance, but the landings were all successful. German troops arriving by air in Tunisia slowed down the Allied moves westwards and by the end of the year a stalemate resulted.

The Russian Campaign

The Russian offensive, begun the previous year, continued with the German forces offering dogged resistance. A period of stalemate followed, for the Russian supply lines were quite lengthy and the Germans had not had sufficient time to organise their own offensive. Eventually, reinforced by poor quality troops, the Germans again moved eastwards and Sebastopol was captured. June saw the opening of the Spring offensives made possible by better weather—Hitler now saw Stalingrad and the Caucasus as his targets.

The last five months of the year witnessed the massive and

decisive battle of Stalingrad as the German armies wilted under a fierce Russian counter-attack. Hitler's change of policy, coupled with his necessary reliance on inferior allied troops, placed his ill-equipped reliable armies in an unenviable position in the face of increasing Russian pressure. The Russians ably demonstrated their great defensive capabilities and, supplied by the Allied Murmansk convoys, began to push the Germans back.

Japanese Pressure

Singapore fell, but the flood of Japanese conquests was partially checked by the naval battles of the Coral Sea and Midway. Thailand was occupied and from there Japanese forces invaded Burma. Slowly the conquest of Burma was achieved, and even the arrival of the soon-to-be famous General Slim in March could not stem the tide. On May 1st Mandalay fell and the British forces retreated into India, Japanese pursuit ceasing at the Imphal river. Pressure was also maintained against the American forces in the Philippines with the taking of Bataan and Corregidor, along with the arrival of Japanese troops in the Solomon and neighbouring islands. The offensive against Papua New Guinea was halted by the doughty defence offered by Australian and American troops. It was seen for the first time that the Japanese could be defeated on a jungle battlefield.

American Counters

Following their successful naval actions, on August 7th the Americans landed marines on Japanese-held Guadalcanal and Tulagi in the Solomon Islands. After some determined and gallant fighting, Guadalcanal was the scene of the first large scale Allied victory against the Japanese. Invaluable experience was gained, which would stand the Americans in good stead for their subsequent 'island hopping' campaign.

Events at Sea

The Germans continued to operate against Allied convoys, both from the United States to the UK and from the UK to Russia. Using U-boats, surface ships and long-range aircraft, the German navy struck hard against merchantmen, particularly off the American east coast. The battleship *Tirpitz* was in Norway, whilst the battle cruisers *Gneisenau* and *Scharnhorst* and the heavy cruiser *Prinz Eugen* dashed up the English Channel from their base in Brest to the North Sea. The Russian convoys were more or less continually harassed and sustained crippling losses. Perhaps the worst hit was convoy PQ-17 losing twenty-three out of an original thirty-seven ships but all suffered terrible losses. Gradually, however, counter measures were developed and the Germans were beginning to lose their U-boats. The Battle of the Atlantic was by no means over, but the tide had certainly turned.

Following the attack on Pearl Harbor, it took some time for the American navy to develop a presence in the Pacific. By good fortune, their three aircraft carriers had not been in the base on the day of the attack and it was around these that a new fleet was hastily formed. By May 1942 the American navy was on the offensive and, in the Battle of the Coral Sea, the first great aircraft carrier engagement and one in which none of the ships on either side actually saw the enemy, forced the Japanese to a draw. A month later, the decisive three-day Battle of Midway cost Japan her carrier fleet and, with it, the naval initiative. This was the main factor in enabling the United States to land marines on Guadalcanal, as mentioned above. The Japanese navy was also active in the Indian Ocean, where they appeared in late March. In a number of actions the British Far Eastern Force suffered heavy losses and were unable to prevent the Japanese First Air Fleet from returning to the Pacific.

The War in the Air

The air war was relatively quiet during this time, but without vital air support many of the actions discussed above could not have taken place. Mention has also been made of the vital part played by carrier-based aircraft in naval battles. May saw the first 1,000 bomber raid mounted by the RAF Bomber Command against the German city of Cologne, causing extensive damage to vital railway installations.

1943

North Africa

The stalemate in Tunisia continued until General Rommel launched a surprise attack to disrupt the Allied plans. The move culminated in a German victory at the Battle of Kasserine Pass in late February. Probing further, Rommel was checked at the Battle of Mareth a month later. Early May saw the start of what was to be the final Allied offensive which, following the battle for Tunisia, saw the demise of the Axis forces.

Sicily

Early June saw General Montgomery's Eighth Army and General Patton's US 7th Army land in Sicily. While initially achieving surprise, the assault slowed in the face of some determined opposition. However, the island was in Allied hands by mid-August.

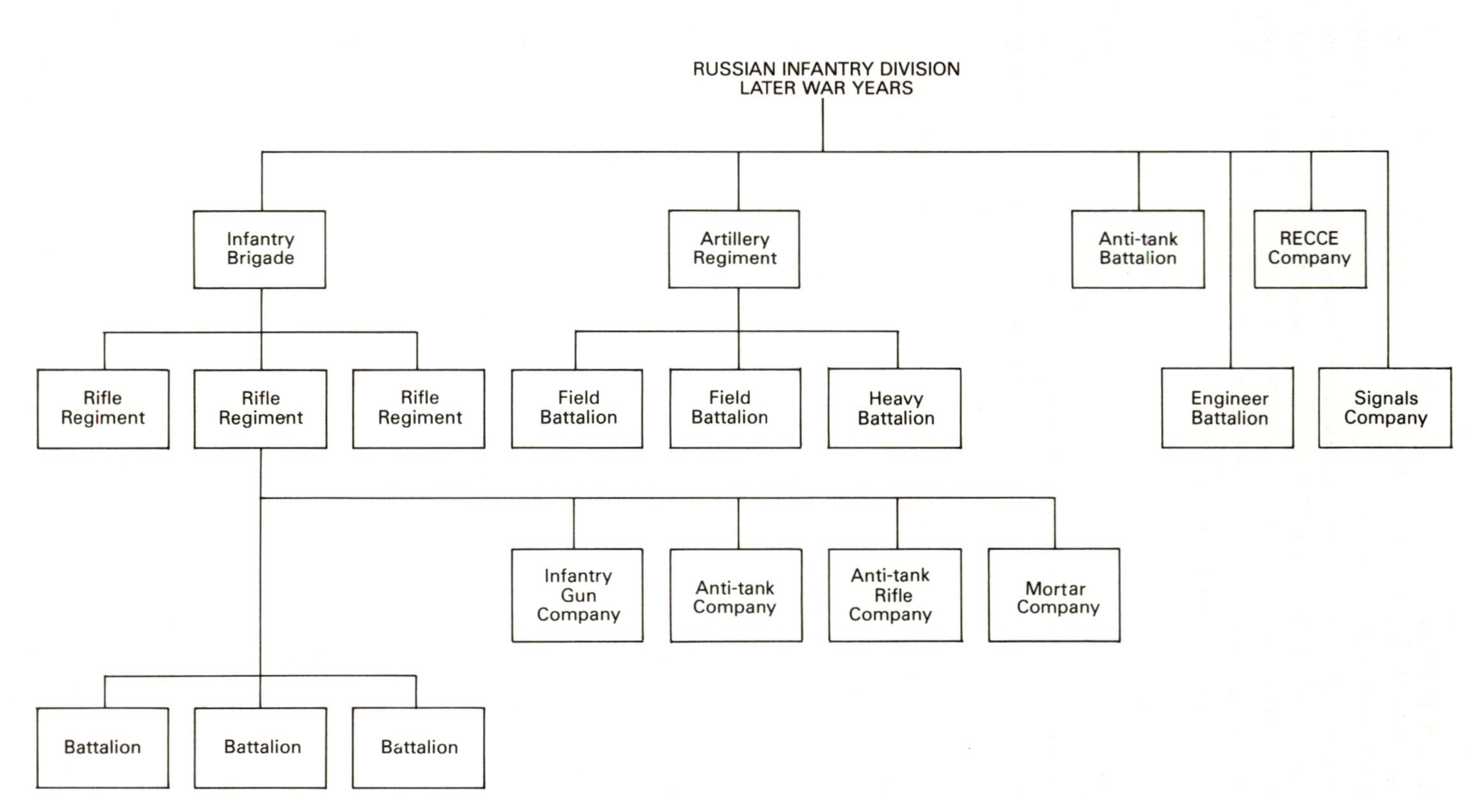

RUSSIAN INFANTRY DIVISION
LATER WAR YEARS
Infantry Brigade
Artillery Regiment
Anti-tank Battalion
RECCE Company
Rifle Regiment
Rifle Regiment
Rifle Regiment
Field Battalion
Field Battalion
Heavy Battalion
Engineer Battalion
Signals Company
Infantry Gun Company
Anti-tank Company
Anti-tank Rifle Company
Mortar Company
Battalion
Battalion
Battalion

The Invasion of Italy

Early the following month, elements of the Eighth Army landed from Sicily on the extreme south of the Italian penisula. The German troops, ably led by Field Marshal Kesselring, put up a very determined resistance and the Allied progress was slow. By the end of the year the advance was halted by Kesselring's formidable Gustav Line which incorporated the monastery at Monte Cassino, the scene of some bitter fighting.

The Eastern Front

The Russians maintained their pressure on the beleaguered German forces, causing the surrender of the Sixth Army in front of Stalingrad. Only some skilfully-conducted countermoves orchestrated by Field Marshal Manstein averted a complete disaster for the Germans but, even so, their offensive abilities were now severely curtailed. A determined, if limited, German counter-thrust in early July resulted in the ultimately indecisive Battle of Kursk, the largest tank battle of the entire war. Hitler, alarmed by the Allied landings in Italy, withdrew some of his armoured divisions from Russia and, from that point onwards, the German forces were on the retreat. The remainder of 1943 was taken up with Russian offensives, massive in size and making full use of their armoured formations. Kharkov, Kiev and Smolensk were all recaptured Even the onset of another Russian winter did not slow down the attacks which pushed the Germans further and further westwards.

Operations in Burma

After reorganising in India, and as a prelude to a larger operation, the Allies launched two unsuccessful minor offensives into Burma, both of which were easily contained by the Japanese. The Allied lack of ability to fight the Japanese in a jungle environment was seen as the key point of these failures. Brigadier General Wingate sought and received permission to try the concept of long-range subversive patrols thrusting deep behind enemy lines. The Chindits, as the soldiers who carried out these actions were called, initially failed in the strict military sense but proved that Allied troops could fight in the jungle. In northern Burma, a Chinese offensive achieved some minor success, but the bulk of the country was still in Japanese hands as the year drew to a close.

The Pacific Theatre

In the south and south-west Pacific, the Japanese, having lost Guadalcanal in the Solomon Islands and Papua, began to tighten their hold on their remaining conquests. Defensively, the key point of these was New Britain in the Bismarck archipelago and it was this island which the American forces sought to take. By late 1943, some partial inroads onto the island had been achieved after some stubborn Japanese resistance had been overcome. At the same time, 'island hopping' was also being successfully conducted in the rest of the Pacific with American and New Zealand troops, all of which lessened the Japanese domination of the area. The taking of Tarawa Atoll, (November 20th–24th), one of the Gilbert Islands in the central Pacific, was one of the bloodiest actions of the war and is rightly quoted as a splendid example of US Marine Corps gallantry and determination in the face of a fanatical defence.

Events at Sea

In the Battle of the Atlantic, the tide had swung against the German U-boats to such an extent that Hitler replaced Admiral Raeder with Admiral Doenitz in an attempt to prevent further Allied successes. Doenitz at once stepped up the pace of the German submarine effort and enjoyed some considerable success as a result. In response to this increase in activity the Allied navies organised groups of vessels, each centered on an aircraft carrier, deliberately to seek out U-boats and sink them. By the end of the year the submarine menace was contained and, due to their heavy losses, the U-boats were never again the threat that they had been in the earlier months. In the early part of 1943 the Russian convoys continued but, with Allied domination in the Mediterranean established, cargoes were sent by way of Iran.

In northern waters the German capital ships *Scharnhorst* and *Tirpitz* continued some minor harassing raids. The *Tirpitz* was crippled after an attack by British midget submarines and, in the Battle of North Cape (December 24th–26th), the *Scharnhorst* was sunk by two Royal Navy task forces.

Without doubt, the land operations in the Solomon Islands were well supported by the American navy in terms of transportation, gunnery support and naval air cover. Also, in a series of cruiser/destroyer actions, the Japanese were defeated on virtually every occasion.

The War in the Air

With Bomber Command of the RAF attacking at night and the American Eighth Air Force during the day, the Allies were now able to maintain continual bombing offensives against German cities and industrial targets. As well as the day/night division, there was also a division in target: the RAF attacked industry and civilian morale by virtue of city bombing, whereas the Americans hit the German aircraft industry along with the Luftwaffe itself. Although the raids were successful, for the morale of the German 'home front' did suffer, industry still carried on and the Luftwaffe became more adept at attacking the often unescorted bomber formations.

It was in the latter half of 1943 that the first rumours of the German V-1 and V-2 secret weapons were beginning to appear. However, accurate bombing missions carried out by the RAF, such as that against Peenemunde in mid-August, considerably delayed the German plans.

As noted above, the support given to operations by American carrier-based aircraft in the Pacific was an important factor. Air superiority, bombing raids, ground attacks, the conveyance of airborne troops and the provision of immediate tactical support, frequently launched from the most improvised local airstrips were all key points for success.

1944

Despite numerous attacks by the RAF and activity by the Resistance, the German V-1 flying bombs began landing on London in mid-June. These were followed by the much more powerful V-2 rockets in September and, while both of these weapons were prevented from landing in huge numbers, those that did were damaging both to property and morale.

In July, German army officers plotted to assassinate Hitler and remove the Nazi regime. The attempt failed and, as a direct result, Hitler assumed control of all things military, removing a number of senior officers from their positions.

Italy

Due to the continuing stalemate on the Gustav Line, the Allies landed troops behind the German lines at Anzio. Due to their subsequent failure to drive inland, the German forces under Kesselring were allowed to build up a strong defence, slowing down the Allied advance. Pressure was maintained against Monte Cassino, however, and finally the Gustav Line was breached in late May. The drive for Rome followed and the city was entered on June 4th. As the year ended, the Allies were in northern Italy facing the next German line of defence, the Gothic Line.

Operation Overlord

Operation *Overlord*—the Allied landings in Occupied Europe—was a gigantic undertaking involving over three million men and their associated equipment. On June 6th, 'D Day', two Allied armies— General Bradley's First US Army and General Dempsey's British Second Army—landed at five beaches in Normandy. The Americans came ashore at Utah and Omaha, while Gold, Juno and Sword witnessed the arrival of the British. An airborne division covered the left, i.e. eastern flank so that, in all, over one million fighting men were put ashore. General Eisenhower was the supreme commander, and the land forces were under the command of General Montgomery, the naval under Admiral Ramsey and the air forces under Air Marshal Sir Leigh-Mallory. Expanding outwards from the beaches was a slow business for the Allies due to the difficult nature of the French countryside. A breakout, Operation *Cobra*, was achieved, and by mid-August some ground had been covered, but the German forces offered a resolute defence which, coupled with some Allied errors, allowed them to fall back and regroup. In mid August, Operation *Anvil-Dragoon* saw French and American troops land in southern France and make significant inroads into the central areas. The Allied advance continued, the River Seine was crossed, Brussels liberated and the vital port of Antwerp taken intact. By mid-September over two million Allied soldiers were advancing eastwards, gathering forces for an attack on Germany itself. As a prelude to this, three airborne divisions were parachuted or transported in gliders to seize three vital bridges over the rivers Lek, Meuse and Rhine. The plan did not work and the Rhine remained in German hands. The Allies continued in their efforts, however, drawing ever closer to the German frontier. In December the Germans counterattacked in the region of the Ardennes in an attempt to split the Allied forces. This unsuccessful move was initially checked and then the Allies themselves countered.

The Eastern Front

Following on from their pressurisation of the German lines, the Russians launched a determined drive against them as the year opened. Well supplied by the Allies, the Russian ground forces moved methodically westwards, despite some skilful defensive fighting by the Germans. In June, just after the Allied landings in France, the Russians launched their largest offensive to date against the thinly-spread German forces. By late September the Mannerheim Line was breached and Finland defeated, the Crimea was re-taken, Poland was occupied and Bulgaria changed sides. On the Baltic coast, it was only on the eastern borders of Germany itself that the Russian drive was halted by German counters in East Prussia. The Danube was reached and German forces in the Balkans only just fought their way out of trouble.

Burma

An advance of three British divisions into northern Burma from India was launched which, despite Japanese opposition, made some headway. The Chinese also continued to pressure the Japanese, but made little headway until the arrival of some American troops ('Merrill's Marauders') bolstered their efforts. In March a second Chindit operation took place, but once again with only very limited success. The American and Chinese advance continued under General Stilwell and made good progress. Following a successful move by British troops under General Festing, General Stilwell—himself replaced in October—initiated a final offensive, the Irrawaddy River being crossed in early November. In central Burma, General Slim's Fourteenth Army had relieved Imphal and Kohima, destroying the Japanese Fifteenth Army in the process. A further advance across the Chidwin River was planned and the end of the year saw this put into operation.

China

The Japanese forces in China launched an offensive in the east of that country which both defeated and pushed back the Chinese forces. The transfer of experienced Chinese troops from Burma was required before the position was stabilised.

The Pacific Theatre

In the south Pacific, the American forces were increasing their hold on the various islands in the area. Western New Guinea became the focus of attention and, as a preliminary, a Japanese base on Hollandia, along with several other strategically important islands, was taken by Australian and American troops in a well-executed operation. In the central Pacific, US marines landed on Saipan after a long, fierce action took the island. Plans were made to retake the Philippines and the first actioned step of these was the landing of troops on Leyte in October. There followed the massive naval battle of Leyte Gulf and the now familiar Japanese opposition on land. The American dominance in the area was now overwhelming the Japanese but they had no thought of surrender.

Events at Sea

The Battle of the Atlantic, particularly vital in the face of the planned Normandy landings, was slowly being won by the Allies. The U-boats were no longer the deadly menace they had once been, although they did achieve some late success, operating from Norway and the Baltic, their bases in France having been lost to them. The most feared surface raider, *Tirpitz*, was sunk whilst undergoing repairs in Norway.

In the Pacific Ocean, the naval war continued. The battle of the Philippine Sea (June 19–21) was the last occasion on which the Japanese navy was able to engage that of the Americans on equal terms. The action saw Japanese naval air power wiped out, for after the battle the Japanese had so few aircraft left that their aircraft carriers—prime weapons in the Pacific naval war—were really of no subsequent use to them. The greatest naval action ever joined, the Battle of Leyte Gulf (October 23–26) was the final battle of the war for the Japanese navy. Its clear defeat in this four-stage action ended its fighting effectiveness.

The War in the Air

The bombing offensive against Germany was continued, with air raids delivered by literally a thousand bombers, a common occurrence. More specialised strategic bombing missions were carried out in direct support of the Normandy landings, both during and after the event. In Burma, the fact that the Japanese could bomb Allied bases with impunity was countered by the arrival of British and American aircraft. By the middle of the year, the Allies dominated the skies over Burma, which greatly assisted their operations on land. American heavy bombers, operating from bases in India, began to attack the Japanese mainland and by the end of the year regular heavy raids were taking place.

1945

Italy

The stalemate centred on the German Gothic Line continued until April, when a combined attack by the British Eighth Army and American Fifth Army finally broke through. German resistance collapsed and the former defenders were continually pushed back until the unconditional surrender, declared from May 2nd.

The War in Europe

As the Allies countered the German offensive in the Ardennes, another German thrust to the north of Strasbourg was contained. During the early months of the year the Rhineland was cleared and the Allies reached the banks of the Rhine. In late March the river was crossed and the Ruhr encircled in what was the last major action of the campaign, ending with the German surrender in early May.

The Eastern Front

The year opened with a Russian attack into eastern Germany and the Danube Valley. On the Baltic coast, huge numbers of German troops were bravely and skilfully evacuated by the German navy as the Russians closed in on their positions. The final offensive against Berlin made contact with Allied troops who were advancing westwards and was successfully concluded by early May.

Burma

In northern Burma, the British and Chinese forces advanced slowly southwards in the face of dogged Japanese resistance, many fiercely-fought actions taking place along the Burma Road. In central Burma, General Slim crossed the Irrawaddy River and captured Mandalay in March. Following the defection of the Burmese army to the British and Allied forces, General Slim launched an attack on Rangoon which was captured in early May. The Japanese forces were pushed into Thailand and, apart from minor skirmishing, there was little fight left in them.

China

The Japanese continued their efforts in south-east China, where they achieved a degree of success. A push into central China however was repulsed by Chinese forces and the Japanese withdrew. As this was going on, the Russians invaded Manchuria and drove the patchy Japanese forces back as far as Korea before the Japanese surrender was announced.

The Pacific Theatre

The Allied re-conquest of the Philippines continued with the attack on the island of Luzon. Slowly the Japanese were driven from their positions, but it was not until early February that the capital Manila was taken, and it was August 15th before the Japanese forces finally surrendered. In New Guinea and its surrounding islands the Australian forces were charged with clearing out the remaining pockets of Japanese resistance, which they did by mid-July. The Pacific island of Iwo Jima was seen as a vital link in the American advance on the Japanese mainland, for which purpose it would serve as an air base. The US marines landed in February and succeeded in taking all the island by mid-March.

The next step before invading Japan was the possession of the Ryukyu group of islands, situated off the southernmost island of Japan. Operation *Iceberg* was planned as an attack on this group, with the largest island, Okinawa, being the principal objective. The US marines landed unopposed on April 1st, but encountered some extremely determined Japanese resistance as they moved inland. Under constant air attack the American troops pushed onwards, containing a determined counterattack as they did so and by the end of June the island was in American hands.

Events at Sea

In January, the German U-boats enjoyed a limited period of success against Allied shipping in the Atlantic, but improved counter-measures ended the submarine menace in early May. Later the same month, the convoy system was scrapped since shipping could by then sail safely on their way. The landings on Iwo Jima were only made possible by the American Fifth Fleet and the invasion of Okinawa, the largest and most complicated amphibious operation of the Pacific war, could not have been undertaken without the protection of the warships. The last Japanese aircraft carrier, *Yamato*, was sunk by American naval aircraft during the action. US submarines effectively blockaded Japan and sank many Japanese vessels as a result.

The War in the Air

The bombing raids on Germany continued against dwindling German defences. The jet-powered Me 262 was put into service to counter the raids, but was not available in sufficiently large numbers to stop the bombers. In mid-February, the city of Dresden was flattened and, by the end of the following month, virtually all the Luftwaffe had been rendered ineffective. American bombers operating from bases in India struck at the Japanese ground force targets, while others, operating from recently captured islands, bombed the Japanese mainland. On August 6th, an atomic bomb was dropped on the city of Hiroshima, followed three days later by another on the seaport of Nagasaki. On August 10th Japan surrendered and the war was over.

Section I–The War on Land

In this chapter we will be looking at the main contenders of the land war, examining their organisation and weaponry. For reasons of space, or rather the lack of same, only the major nations which were involved will be covered, but these should satisfy by far the greater part of the wargamer's needs.

ORGANISATION

The details concerning the organisation of a country's forces are of particular interest to the wargamer, for it is on this historical basis that model armies are invariably constructed. However, the recording of such organisations is not too easy to achieve. The establishments varied from nation to nation, theatre to theatre, and campaign to campaign. Further, temporary formations were often hastily assembled for a particular task, disbanded, re-formed or amalgamated with others, and so forth. A prime example of this is the battle-group, a formation frequently employed by the German army and varying in size from 100 or 200 men up to several thousand. Even ignoring this *ad hoc* type of arrangement, lucky indeed was the commander who had, firstly, all the units allocated to him on paper and, secondly, formations which were anything like up to strength.

As a result of this, the wargamer must be prepared to apply only loosely any of the organisational details provided, for they will frequently be the theoretical rather than the actual establishments. That said, the table top general has to start somewhere and, if one's model forces can be brought up to establishment levels which their historical forebears failed to achieve, then so be it!

Australia
Australia needed two land forces: one for home defence and a second for overseas service, where Australian soldiers fought with distinction in the North African, Far Eastern and Mediterranean theatres, proving to be some of the toughest Allied formations. The

An assortment of Partisan figures.

Russian Infantry. (This, and the following sequence of photographs courtesy of Platoon 20).

Russian infantry in a variety of uniforms and action poses.

A heavy 120mm Russian mortar with its crew of two.

first unit of war-bound fighting troops raised in Australia was termed the 6th division—there were already five militia formations for home defence in the 1st Australian Imperial Force (AIF)—and was formed from volunteers from within the ranks of that militia. Initially, the AIF division was organised into three infantry brigades, each composed of four battalions. These were supported by artillery regiments and a mechanised reconnaissance regiment.

Following the fall of France in 1940, the Australian government sanctioned the raising of three further infantry AIF divisions, 7th, 8th and 9th. There was no shortage of recruits and, by early 1941, three divisions, 6th (16th, 17th and 19th brigades), 7th (18th, 21st and 25th brigades) and 7th (20th, 24th and 26th brigades) were serving in the Middle East, while the 8th went to Malaya. Although the 8th division was very active in Indonesia and Malaya, most of the Australian war effort was directed (in co-operation with the American forces) to the South West Pacific where, by 1944, they were grouped as two corps. Of these two formations, I corps had 6th, 7th and 9th divisions, whilst II corps was composed of the 3rd, 5th and 11th militia divisions of the New Guinea Force.

In summary, the four AIF divisions were composed thus:
6th Division 16th Brigade 2/1st, 2/2nd, 2/3rd Battalions
17th Brigade 2/5th, 2/6th, 2/7th Battalions
19th Brigade 2/4th, 2/8th, 2/11th Battalions
7th Division 18th Brigade 2/9th, 2/1st, 2/12th Battalions
21st Brigade 2/14th, 2/16th, 2/27th Battalions
25th Brigade 2/25th, 2/31st, 2/33rd Battalions
8th Division 22nd Brigade 2/18th, 2/19th, 2/20th Battalions
23rd Brigade 2/21st, 2/22nd, 2/40th Battalions
27th Brigade 2/26th, 2/29th, 2/30th Battalions
9th Division 20th Brigade 2/13th, 2/15th, 2/17th Battalions
24th Brigade 2/28th, 2/32nd, 2/43rd Battalions
26th Brigade 2/23rd, 2/24th, 2/48th Battalions
(Note that the prefix "2/" was used to indicate AIF foreign service, as opposed to militia, formations.)

Each infantry division had its own armour, artillery, engineers, signals, service corps, medical corps and provost company. In addition there were a number of non-divisional formations, eight Independent companies, and eleven Commando squadrons, while four machine gun battalions and the same number of Pioneer battalions provided the Corps troops. Each battalion had a headquarters company of six platoons—administration/transport, anti-aircraft, carrier (equipped with ten Universal Carriers armed with Bren light machine guns), mortar (armed with two 3″ mortars), pioneer and signals—and four rifle companies each of three platoons, each in turn consisting of three sections. Each section had a Bren light

A section of Russian engineers equipped with a flame-thrower in addition to hand-held and dog-carried anti-tank weapons.

machine gun, a 2″ mortar and possibly a Boys anti-tank rifle. Each division had a mechanized carrier regiment kitted out with 48 Universal Carriers armed with Brens and Boys anti-tank rifles, and 28 light tanks, each armed with two machine guns. The artillery regiments had two batteries, each consisting of twelve 25 pounder gun-howitzers, and the divisional anti-tank regiments were equipped with 2 pounders. The capabilities of all these weapons, as with all those in the following paragraphs, will be covered in the next part of this book which deals with the weaponry of the various contenders.

Canada

The Canadian Active Service Force (CASF), as the Canadian expeditionary force was termed, was unique in that it consisted entirely of volunteers. Eventually, the CASF in England prior to Operation *Overlord* grew to include the 1st, 2nd and 3rd infantry divisions, the 1st and 2nd army tank brigades and the 4th and 5th armoured divisions. For much of the early war years, the CASF was a garrison force in England, but the Royal Rifles of Canada and the Winnipeg Grenadiers were sent to Hong Kong in 1941, the 2nd division were involved in the raid on Dieppe in 1942 and then Canadian forces became involved in virtually every theatre. As with the Australian forces, the order of battle of the CASF as assembled for D-Day is fairly short and, since this offers a rare opportunity to record a complete run down, it is listed, for interest, in full.

1st infantry division
Divisional troops: 4th Reconnaissance Regiment
(4th Princess Louise Dragoon Guards)
The Royal Canadian Artillery
The Saskatoon Light Infantry (machine guns)

1st infantry brigade: The Royal Canadian Regiment
                           The Hastings & Prince Edward Regiment
                           The 48th Highlanders of Canada
2nd infantry brigade: The Princess Patricia's Canadian Lt. Inf
                           The Seaforth Highlanders of Canada
                           The Loyal Edmonton Regiment
3rd infantry brigade: The Royal 22nd Regiment
                           The Carleton and York Regiment
                           The West Nova Scotia Regiment

2nd infantry division
Divisional troops: 8th Reconnaissance Regiment
                           (14th Canadian Hussars)
                           The Royal Canadian Artillery
                           The Toronto Scottish Regiment (machine
                           guns)
4th infantry brigade: The Royal Regiment of Canada
                           The Royal Hamilton Light Infantry
                           The Essex Scottish Regiment
5th infantry brigade: The Black Watch of Canada
                           The Regiment de Maisonneuve
                           The Calgary Highlanders
6th infantry brigade: Les Fusiliers Mont-Royal
                           The Queen's Own Cameron Highlanders
                           of Canada
                           The South Saskatchewan Regiment

3rd infantry division
Divisional troops: 7th Reconnaissance Regiment
                           (17th Duke of York's Royal Canadian
                           Hussars)
                           The Royal Canadian Artillery
                           The Cameron Highlanders of Ottawa
                           (machine guns)

German infantry men equipped with a variety of weapons.

7th infantry brigade:	The Royal Winnipeg Rifles
	The Regina Rifle Regiment
	1st Canadian Scottish
8th infantry brigade:	The Queen's Own Rifles of Canada
	The Regiment de la Chaudière
	The North Shore (New Brunswick) Regt.
9th infantry brigade:	The Highland Light Infantry of Canada
	The Stormont, Dundas & Glengarry Highlanders
	The North Nova Scotia Highlanders

4th armoured division

Divisional troops:	29th Armoured Reconnaissance Regiment (The South Alberta Regiment)
	The Royal Canadian Artillery
4th armoured brigade:	21st Armoured Regiment (The Governor General's Foot Guards)
	22nd Armoured Regiment (The Canadian Grenadier Guards)
	28th Armoured Regiment (The British Columbia Regiment)
	The Lake Superior Regiment
10th infantry brigade:	The Lincoln and Welland Regiment
	The Algonquin Regiment
	The Argyll and Sutherland Highlanders of Canada

5th armoured division

Divisional troops:	3rd Armoured Reconnaissance Regiment (The Governor General's Horse Guards)
	The Royal Canadian Artillery
5th armoured brigade:	2nd Armoured Regiment (Lord Strathcona's Horse)
	5th Armoured Regiment (8th Princess Louise's (New Brunswick) Hussars)
	9th Armoured Regiment (The British Columbia Dragoons)
	The Westminster Regiment
11th infantry brigade:	The Perth Regiment
	The Cape Breton Highlanders
	The Irish Regiment of Canada
1st armoured brigade:	11th Armoured Regiment (The Ontario Regiment)
	12th Armoured Regiment

German paratroopers (*Fallschirmjagers*).

The German MG42 machine gun.

A section of Russian infantrymen.

German infantry.

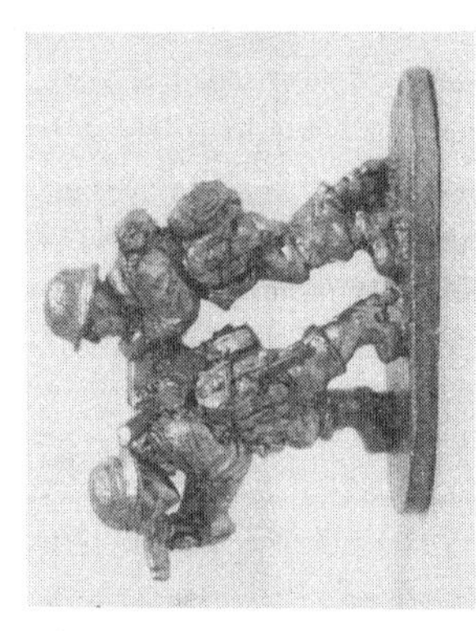

A selection of German paratroop types.

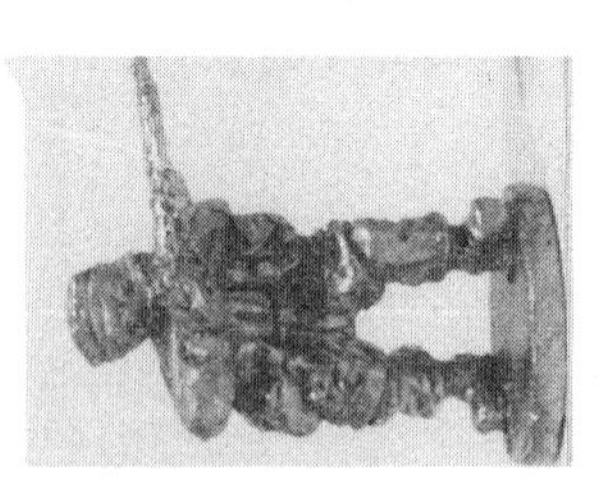

A German paratrooper.   A German two man machine gun crew.

	(Three Rivers Regiment)
	14th Armoured Regiment
	(The Calgary Regiment)
2nd armoured brigade:	6th Armoured Regiment
	(1st Hussars)
	10th Armoured Regiment
	(The Fort Garry Horse)
	27th Armoured Regiment
	(The Sherbrook Fusiliers)

Mention should also be made of the 1st Canadian Parachute Battalion which dropped as part of the 6th British Airborne Division on D-Day. The CASF armoured divisions largely tended to adopt the British organisation of one armoured and one infantry brigade, but the 5th division was at variance with this. In the later years of the war, the Canadian army became very cosmopolitan, with American, British, Czechoslovakian, Dutch and Polish units being contained within its ranks. The ideal force perhaps, for the wargamer who likes variety in a table top army!

China

The Chinese Nationalist Army, in co-operation with the Communist army of Mao Tse-Tung, assisted the Allied war effort by tying down huge numbers of Japanese troops following that nation's attempted conquest of China. Led by Chiang Kai-shek and several war committees, the Chinese Nationalists suffered from a fair degree of disruption, brought about by petty disagreements and power struggles between commanders. An infantry division was a heterogeneous organisation with a nominal strength of just over 9,000, but more typically mustering 6,000 to 7,000. In addition to being poorly trained and relatively inefficient, the divisions also lacked heavy equipment and artillery. Apparently, Chiang Kai-shek kept most of the artillery pieces to himself, apart from handing out some to his favoured commanders in return for a show of loyalty or whatever!

As a result, the trench mortar was the chief support weapon—a division could have anywhere between 18 and 30 of them. The mortars were supplemented by a fair number of light machine guns (typically 200 per division) and heavy machine guns (36 per division). It is interesting to note that the arrival of American aid did not alleviate the problem—such weapons were taken and hoarded by the commanding officers of the divisions. Usually three infantry regiments made up a division, and an army (there were no corps formations) would have three divisions. Three such armies would form a group army, led by a local warlord—overall strategy was not commonplace in Chinese military thinking. There were a number of other formations, such as the 30 divisions which Chiang Kai-shek retained under his personal command to ensure the loyalty of his field commanders and to keep an eye on the Communist forces.

France

The French army was the second largest in the world in 1940, but in reality there are three French armies to consider—the Regular Army of 1940, the Free French and the Vichy Metropolitan army.

Regular Army

The French regular army was a conscript force which enjoyed the presence of a fair number of regular soldiers. Infantry and Alpine divisions were composed of three infantry regiments, each of three battalions, supported by two artillery regiments which provided 36 field guns and 24 medium pieces. Integral to the division were 52 light anti-tank guns and in addition there was a reconnaissance squadron, two engineer companies and the usual supportive elements. Fortress divisions consisted of only the infantry regiments. A cavalry division consisted of two horsed and one mechanised regiment, a reconnaissance group, 12 field guns, 12 medium pieces, eight 47mm anti-tank guns, 20 light tanks and finally, 15 armoured cars. A mechanised division had two regiments of tanks, each consisting of 87 light or medium tanks, a reconnaissance regiment of 40 armoured cars and three motorised infantry battalions.

Artillery support was provided by 24 field guns, 12 medium guns and nine 47mm anti-tank guns. Armoured divisions had two light and two medium tank regiments giving 62 medium and 84 light tanks, an infantry battalion in armoured carriers and an artillery regiment, equipped with twenty-four 105mm field pieces. Integrally, there were 167 anti-tank guns. In addition to the armoured divisons, there were a number of independent tank battalions which were allocated at army level. Most French formations contained a mixture of active regulars, conscripts and reservists of which there were two groups, dependent on age. The French colonial forces tended to be composed largely of regulars, both French and native.

The Free French

The Free French Forces rallying to Charles de Gaulle consisted largely of units from France's Army of Africa. Eventually, the First French army, as the Free French became, consisted of three armoured and nine infantry divisions. In addition there were three Moroccan 'Tabor' groups and some independent commando formations.

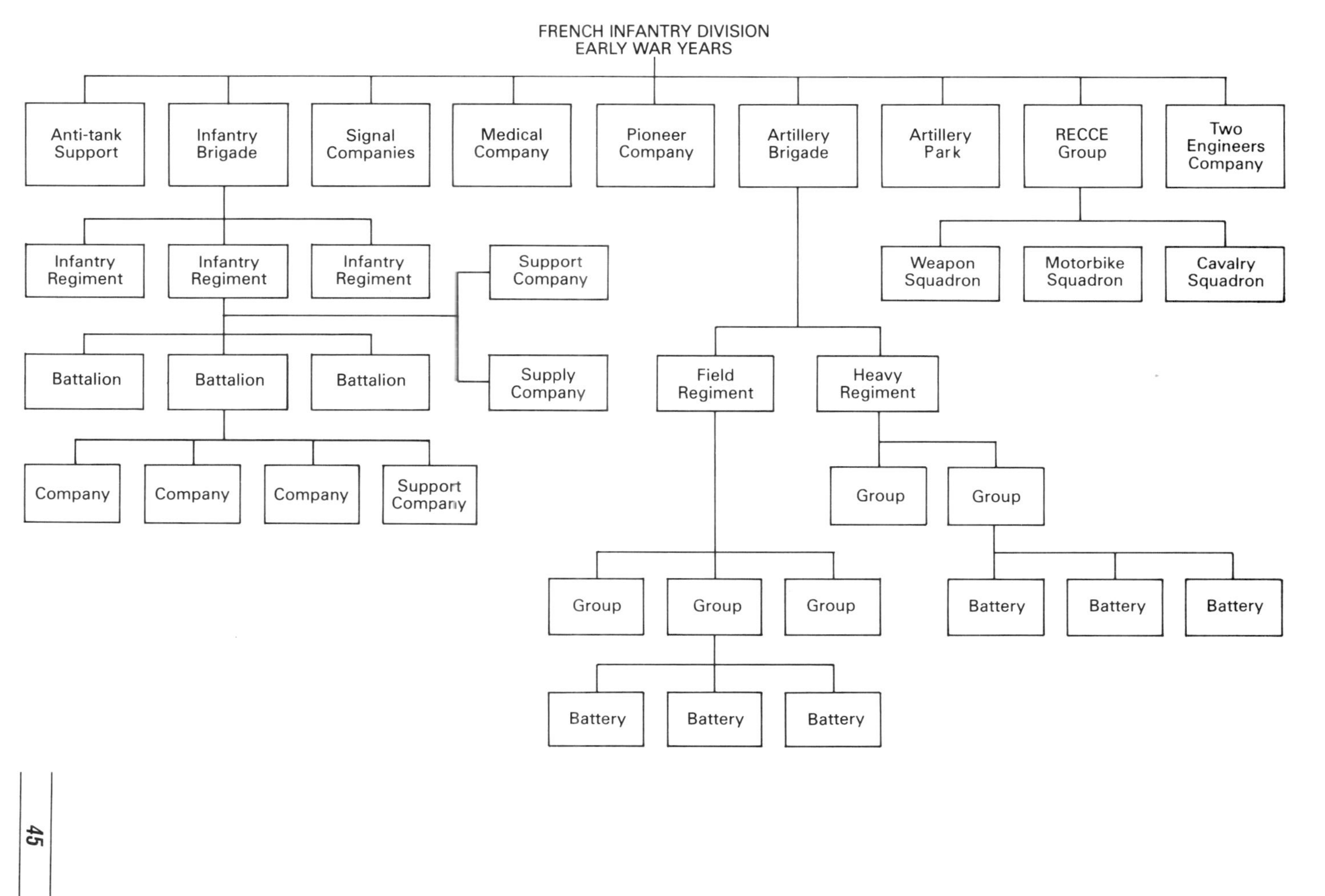

FRENCH INFANTRY DIVISION
EARLY WAR YEARS
Anti-tank Support
Infantry Brigade
Signal Companies
Medical Company
Pioneer Company
Artillery Brigade
Artillery Park
RECCE Group
Two Engineers Company
Infantry Regiment
Infantry Regiment
Infantry Regiment
Support Company
Supply Company
Weapon Squadron
Motorbike Squadron
Cavalry Squadron
Battalion
Battalion
Battalion
Field Regiment
Heavy Regiment
Company
Company
Company
Support Company
Group
Group
Group
Group
Group
Group
Battery
Battery
Battery
Battery
Battery
Battery

The Vichy Metropolitan Army

The Vichy Metropolitan Army was divided into two groups, each of four divisions and was composed of 18 infantry, 11 cavalry (motorised) and eight artillery regiments, and 15 Chasseur battalions. The army had no armoured formations, having had all their vehicles taken away.

Germany

For some reason, which has never been totally explained to my satisfaction, the German army is by far the most popular with wargamers. There is a massive amount of information available but, paradoxically, this tends to cause more problems than it solves, for one feels virtually obliged to record every change in organisation as this information is so readily to hand. In the pursuit of happy compromise, the main changes in organisation will be recorded here, with some additional remarks where pertinent.

On mobilisation, there were 51 active divisions in the German army—35 infantry, four motorised (Panzer grenadier), five armoured or Panzer (plus a brigade), four light and three mountain. For the Polish campaign two army groups were created: army group north was divided into two armies each of three corps, and the southern group was composed of ten corps in three armies. Army group north had one Panzer, one mixed army/SS, two motorised and 16 infantry divisions and a cavalry brigade. In the southern group were four Panzer, four light, 21 infantry and three mountain divisions.

Infantry divisions

By May 1940, the German army consisted of 129 infantry divisions, ten armoured, four motorised, four light motorised, three mountain and one cavalry division. The German airforce (Luftwaffe) contributed a parachute division and there were also three Waffen (armed) SS divisions. Following the battle of France, some infantry divisions were reduced, but more were raised for the invasion of Russia in 1941 and numbers tended to increase until the tide turned three years later. Some infantry divisions—there were eventually over 300—were converted to either Panzer or Panzer grenadier formations. Eventually, the Luftwaffe managed to field one panzer, ten infantry and ten parachute divisions. The Waffen SS raised over 30 divisions, but less than half of these were up to full strength. Initially, infantry divisions had three infantry regiments, each of which was three battalions strong. Attached to the divisions were a reconnaissance squadron, an anti-tank battalion, an engineer battalion and an artillery regiment of nine batteries equipped with 105mm howitzers, and three kitted out with 150mm howitzers.

A 'G.I.' the American infantry man of World War Two.

American infantrymen, equipped with automatic weapons.

Towards the end of the war, the infantry regiments had only two battalions and the artillery support had been reduced from 48 guns to 32, although better anti-tank and anti-aircraft equipment was available by then. An increasing number of foreign troops served in the German army as the war progressed. Men from the Baltic States—Estonia, Latvia and Lithuania—Croatia, France, Italy, Serbia, Slovakia, Spain and the Soviet Union were all found in German or German-controlled formations. The motorised divisions initially had a battalion of tanks, three infantry and one motorised artillery regiment, but one regiment was removed from the establishment as more Panzer divisions were formed. The organisation and strength of the armoured formations altered radically as the war progressed. In 1940 an armoured division mustered 328 tanks, five motorised infantry battalions, engineer, anti-tank and reconnaissance battalions and six artillery batteries providing twenty-four 150mm howitzers. By 1944 a full strength establishment (the exception, by this time, rather than the rule) allowed for 159 tanks, and four motorised infantry battalions.

While also constantly changing their establishment, infantry regiments possessed their own headquarters, with a staff company and bicycle, engineer and signals platoons. In the battalions, there were initially three rifle companies, a machine-gun company, heavy machine-gun and heavy mortar platoons. The rifle companies contained an anti-tank rifle squad. The heavy machine gun platoon had two weapons, each with a crew of 12, whilst the mortar platoon had three sections, each of 19 men and two 8.1cm mortars.

Later regiments dispensed with the separate machine gun formations and instead fielded four rifle companies with integral heavy weapon units. By the end of 1943, the division consisted of three infantry regiments, each about 2,000 men and two battalions strong, supported by an artillery regiment of three field artillery battalions and one of medium artillery and the usual anti-tank,

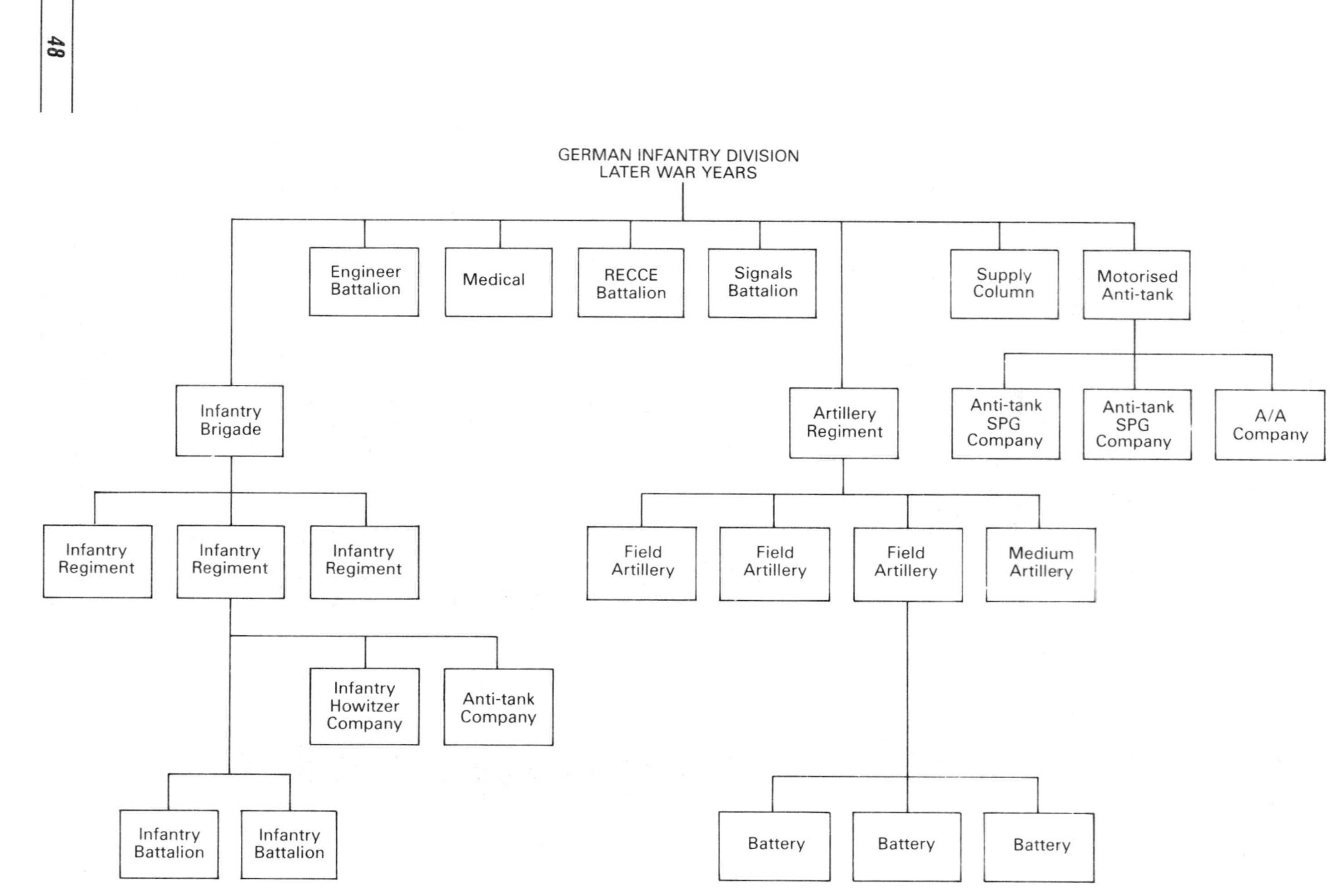

GERMAN INFANTRY DIVISION
LATER WAR YEARS
Engineer Battalion
Medical
RECCE Battalion
Signals Battalion
Supply Column
Motorised Anti-tank
Infantry Brigade
Artillery Regiment
Anti-tank SPG Company
Anti-tank SPG Company
A/A Company
Infantry Regiment
Infantry Regiment
Infantry Regiment
Field Artillery
Field Artillery
Field Artillery
Medium Artillery
Infantry Howitzer Company
Anti-tank Company
Infantry Battalion
Infantry Battalion
Battery
Battery
Battery

signals, medical, engineer, reconnaissance and supply elements. By 1944 the battalion mustered just over 700 men and was usually divided into three rifle companies of 140 men and a 200 strong heavy weapons company.

Artillery formations

The artillery regiment attached to the infantry divisions was divided into three field artillery companies, each of which had three 4 gun batteries of 10.5cm gun-howitzers. Initially, the medium artillery was a company attached to the division rather than being the integral part it later became. At both army and corps level there were additional heavy and medium artillery batteries available, ranging from the 8.8cm to the massive 60cm. The Germans tended to allocate their artillery to the infantry formations. It was not until late in 1943 that the artillery division came into being, inspired by the Soviet use of similar formations. The division had three mixed regiments, each of three battalions with supporting infantry and anti-tank units.

Panzer divisions

Armoured divisions started the war with two tank regiments each of two battalions. Each battalion had four companies, which in turn mustered 32 tanks, giving a theoretical total of 561 tanks, including reserves and so forth. The actual figure in the field, however, was nearer to 300. By 1941–42 the panzer division had 150–200 tanks in one regiment of two or three battalions, each of three companies and a panzer-grenadier brigade of one, two, or rarely three battalions. These were supported by an artillery regiment and the standard support units, including re-enforced anti-tank and reconnaissance elements.

By 1944 the panzer divisions were organised as a tank regiment of two 4 company battalions, each with 48 tanks. The artillery regiment had a battalion of twelve 10.5cm and six 15cm self-propelled guns, a battalion of two 10.5cm howitzer batteries (each of six pieces) and a third battalion of three 15cm howitzer batteries (each of four). The panzer-grenadiers consisted of two regiments, one of which had 7.5cm self-propelled guns. The first battalion of each regiment was mounted in half-tracks, whilst the second travelled in lorries. Each regiment had a company of six 15cm self-propelled guns and a pioneer company.

Weapons will be covered in a separate section, but it was the introduction of the Mark VI Tiger Tank which brought about the next change. Separate battalions of Tigers were deployed under the direct control of the area or battlefield commander. The battalions mustered 45 tanks which were divided into four companies, with support units including an anti-aircraft unit with twelve 2cm guns.

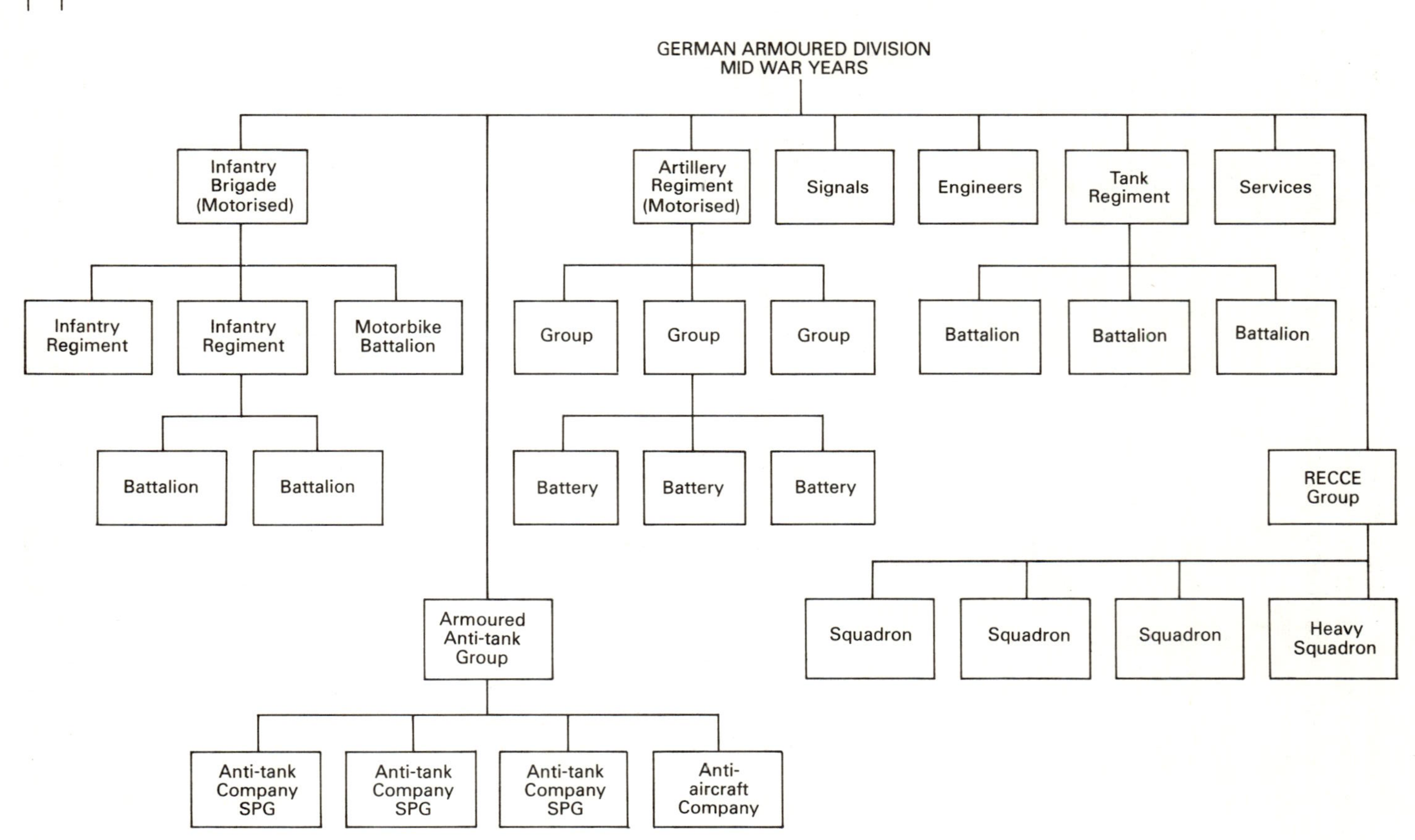

GERMAN ARMOURED DIVISION
MID WAR YEARS
Infantry Brigade (Motorised)
Artillery Regiment (Motorised)
Signals
Engineers
Tank Regiment
Services
Infantry Regiment
Infantry Regiment
Motorbike Battalion
Group
Group
Group
Battalion
Battalion
Battalion
Battalion
Battalion
Battery
Battery
Battery
RECCE Group
Squadron
Squadron
Squadron
Heavy Squadron
Armoured Anti-tank Group
Anti-tank Company SPG
Anti-tank Company SPG
Anti-tank Company SPG
Anti-aircraft Company

The final change in the establishment of the panzer divisions took place in 1945 and reduced the tank regiment to 50 vehicles, but it is questionable as to whether or not this was implemented before the German surrender.

Light divisions

The relatively short-lived light divisions were basically motorised cavalry formations and varied in organisation. A fairly typical set-up would be a light tank battalion, one, perhaps two cavalry rifle regiments each having two or three battalions, a motorised artillery regiment of 24 gun-howitzers, an anti-tank battalion (equipped with thirty-six 10.5cm, twelve 2cm) and either a motorised reconnaissance battalion or an armoured car regiment. The original four light divisions were converted to armoured divisions after the Polish campaign— some infantry divisions were designated as 'light', but these were essentially still organised as infantry formations.

Mountain troops

Due to their relatively unusual nature, the élitist mountain divisions are always interesting to look at. Similar in many ways to the organisation of the infantry divisions, the mountain troops were quite flexible in their establishments. Typically, there were two infantry regiments, each of three battalions, each of which in turn had five companies. The artillery regiment had two battalions of eight 7.5cm guns, one of eight 10.5cm and a fourth of eight 15cm. The anti-tank battalion featured 24 motorised 3.7cm guns and there were also two regimental companies each equipped with nine 3.7cm and three 4.7cm pieces.

Cavalry formations

The German army was, predictably enough, low on cavalry. As an aside, it is interesting to note that even in the Second World War, a conflict often thought of as highly mechanised, great use was made of horse-powered transport. The bulk of the German artillery, for example, was horsedrawn throughout the war. The initial solitary cavalry brigade had two mounted regiments supported by a battery of mounted artillery. The regiments had four squadrons and a support or heavy squadron, equipped with six 8cm mortars and four 7.5cm guns. After the Polish campaign, the cavalry was expanded to a full division by the addition of a second brigade.

Airborne Forces

The German airborne forces were under the control of Hermann Goering and his Luftwaffe. While they did carry out some well-executed airborne operations, the bulk of the employment of the

(Above): U.S. infantry figures. (Left): A lone American infantryman on patrol.

airborne forces was as infantry. The 7th division which spearheaded the attack on Crete in May 1941 was organised into three regiments, each of three battalions. Attached were air signals, anti-tank, medical and transport companies, light anti-aircraft and pak batteries and a motor cycle platoon. The General Goering regiment of parachutists was eventually expanded into a brigade in the summer of 1942, when it consisted of a grenadier regiment, a jager regiment, an anti-aircraft regiment and supporting elements. Later that same year it was further enlarged to full divisional strength with a regiment of panzers, two of panzer-grenadiers and one of artillery, as well as full supporting elements, including an anti-aircraft regiment. There were also numerous, less glamorous Luftwaffe field divisions who did not perform too well. In all as many as 22 field divisions were raised and they varied dramatically in size and organisation.

Waffen SS

Starting life as Hitler's Staff Guard (Schutzstaffel (SS)—Stabs-wache), becoming a complete regiment Bodyguard Regiment Adolf Hitler (Leibstandarte SS Adolf Hitler), Waffen SS units formed an integral part of army formations, but gradually they formed their own divisions. The difficulty in finding recruits caused the leader of the SS, Heinrich Himmler, to look to occupied countries for manpower. At the time of Operation *Barbarossa*, the SS fielded Das Reich, Polizei, Totenkopf and Wiking divisions, Leibstandarte Adolf Hitler brigade, the battlegroup Nord and an infantry regiment. Baltic State, Belgian, Croatian, Danish, Dutch, French and Norwegian troops all served in the SS at some stage of the war.

By early 1945 there were 38 Waffen SS divisions, but many were understrength and not at combat readiness. It is tempting to list the component units of the divisions, for the major units—Das Reich, Leibstandarte Adolf Hitler, Totenkopf etc., certainly appeal to wargamers, as do the cavalry division 'Florian Gever', the largely Hitler youth 'Hitlerjugend' and the Waffen Gebirgs Division der SS 'Handschar' (Kroatische Nr1) which was recruited from Bosnian Moslems and kitted out in German uniforms and fezzes. We could however, take one SS Panzer division—'Wiking'—as an example. In 1944 the division consisted of the 5th SS Panzer regiment, the 9th 'Germania' SS Panzer-grenadier and the 10th 'Westland' SS Panzer-grenadier regiment.

The Afrika Korps

General Rommel's Afrika Korps was originally partially formed from the 5th Light Division, later designated the 21st Panzer. The units were the 5th Panzer regiment of two strong tank battalions totalling 150 tanks, 104th (motorised) infantry regiment consisting of two panzer-grenadier battalions, 3rd (motorised) reconnaissance battalion, two strong anti-tank battalions and an artillery battalion. This formation was reinforced initially by the 15th panzer division and subsequently by the 90th Light Division, two Italian Corps (XX and XXI) and the Savona division, also Italian. As a result, the Afrika Korps became Panzer Group Afrika and then in 1942 after being supplemented, the 164th infantry division and the Ramcke Parachute Brigade, became Panzer Army Afrika. Also known as the German/Italian Panzer Army, it became the 1st Italian Army in February 1943 and was combined with the 5th Panzer Army to form Army Group Afrika, the last grouping of the Axis forces in North Africa.

By March 1943 the 5th Panzer Army consisted of the 10th panzer division—7th panzer, 69th and 86th panzer-grenadiers, 21st panzer division—5th panzer, 104th panzer-grenadiers, 334th infantry division—three motorised panzer-grenadier regiments (754, 755 and 756), 999th infantry division (composed of court-martialled German soldiers) and division von Manteuffel, which was a mixed parachute and panzer-grenadier outfit. Infantry division Superga, Brigade Imperiali and the 19th and 20th anti-aircraft divisions completed the line up.

Volksgrenadiers

Volksgrenadier divisions came into being late in 1944, many of them being organised from the remnants of divisions decimated in battle. In all, 50 such divisions were created, organised as three 2 battalion regiments and an artillery regiment of twenty-four 10.5 cm howitzers, twelve 15cm howitzers and eighteen 7.5cm guns. In

British infantry of World War Two.

A selection of British infantry figures.

support was an anti-tank battalion, an engineer battalion and a signals battalion.

Italy

In 1940, Italy possessed 59 infantry, six alpine, a similar number of mobile (celere), two motorised and three armoured divisions. Few of these formations, however, were up to their full establishments, either in men or equipment. Although the division was the main structure of the Italian army, a number of units were assigned at corps or at army level as a reserve.

The Infantry Division

The infantry division was based on two regiments and from March 1940 a two battalion legion of fascist troops was included in the regular army formations. The division was composed of a headquarters (336), two infantry regiments (3279 each), a mortar battalion (435), a pack gun company (241), a divisional artillery regiment (2769), an engineer battalion (440) and the fascist Blackshirt Legion (1693). There were the usual divisional support functions and sometimes a reserve infantry battalion. The infantry regiment usually had three rifle battalions, although there could be as many as five in some formations. The battalion had 876 men organised into a headquarters company, three rifle companies and a support arms company of two machine gun platoons each of four heavy machine guns and two 45mm mortar platoons with nine mortars each. The 156 man strong companies were divided into a headquarters platoon and three rifle sections, each of two sections. The two Blackshirt battalions were organised along similar lines, but were only 700 men strong. In their case the support company had two machine gun platoons each with three machine guns and two mortar platoons, each with three 81mm mortars.

The regiment of artillery consisted of a regimental headquarters, a horsedrawn 100mm howitzer battery, another horsedrawn battery of 75mm guns, a 75mm reserve howitzer battery—36 pieces in all—and a mechanised 20mm anti-aircraft troop. Each battery was of three troops each of four pieces, whilst the anti-aircraft troop had four sections, each of two guns. A mortar battalion had three companies each armed with six 81mm mortars, whilst a gun company had eight 47mm guns divided into four platoons. In the divisions designated as mountain formations, the organisation was the same as for the line, apart from the artillery which had three 75mm batteries of howitzers, each of three troops. All these were either pack transportable or could be carried in horsedrawn wagons.

The Alpini

The true mountain troops, the Alpini, differed rather more from the regular organisation. The support elements were permanently attached to regiments, a fact which made such formations self-supporting and thus able to operate alone—a useful facility in mountain warfare. After the divisional headquarters of 388 men including the anti-tank platoon, there were two Alpine regiments each 4757, the divisional artillery regiment (1710) of two 75mm howitzer batteries, an engineer battalion (341), a chemical warfare company (234), two reserve battalions at 766 men each and the supports—medical, supply and transport totalling some 1500 in all. Regiments had the usual headquarters company which included a platoon of flame-throwers, three Alpine battalions each 1267 men formed into three companies (each 340 men and a machine gun platoon) with medical, supply and transport services. The two divisional artillery 75mm batteries were split between the two Alpine regiments, with three troops of each battery being allocated to each battalion.

North African Formations

In an attempt to increase the firepower and mobility of the division, a new organisation was introduced in 1942 for North Africa. Now a division had two regiments of infantry, one of artillery and a mixed engineer battalion with services. The size of the infantry regiment was variable, based as it was on the two to four company battalion, with two or three battalions to a regiment. A regiment with say three battalions, each of four companies would muster something over 2,000 men. The artillery had one or two 12 gun 100mm batteries, supported by a troop armed with eight 20mm guns. Mechanised divisions were created from infantry divisions, but apart from gaining more mortars and losing the Blackshirts, the organisation did not change for the transition. Those divisions that had been motor transportable were upgraded to motorised for North Africa and organised as two infantry regiments, each of two infantry battalions, a support and anti-tank battalion which included anti-aircraft, anti-tank, machine gun and mortar companies, an artillery regiment, a light tank battalion of 46 tanks, divisional support, an anti-tank battalion and finally an engineer battalion. The tank battalion had a headquarters of seven tanks and three companies each having 13 tanks.

Bersaglieri

The true motorised division was of the North Africa type, but benefited from the inclusion of a Bersaglieri regiment. Such formations consisted of 1827 élite riflemen organised into a

Vickers Light Mark VI Tanks in France 1940.

headquarters company, a motorcycle company, two lorry-borne battalions, a support and anti-aircraft battalion. Each Bersaglieri battalion had a headquarters company, two rifle companies plus a support and anti-tank company.

The Mobile Divisions
The mobile divisions were the descendants of the former cavalry regiments and were intended as reconnaissance or support, sacrificing as they did, firepower for speed. Such divisions had two cavalry regiments, a three battalion Bersaglieri regiment, a Bersaglieri motorcycle company, an anti-tank company, a divisional artillery regiment, a light tank group of 61 tanks (in four squadrons) and a mixed engineer company.

The Armoured Divisions
The armoured divisions were reorganised and up-gunned during the war. A division had a tank regiment of three to five battalions, each of 55 tanks, a mechanised artillery regiment of two 12 gun 75mm batteries, one 18 gun 105mm battery, one eight gun 90mm battery and two self-propelled ten gun batteries. To support the artillery there was a troop of 47mm anti-tank guns and three anti-aircraft troops armed with 20mm guns. Also in the division, a support and anti-tank battalion, a mixed engineer company and a Bersaglieri regiment.

Airborne Forces
Although not strong on paratroop units, the Italians raised two divisions of them. Each division was of two regiments, each having

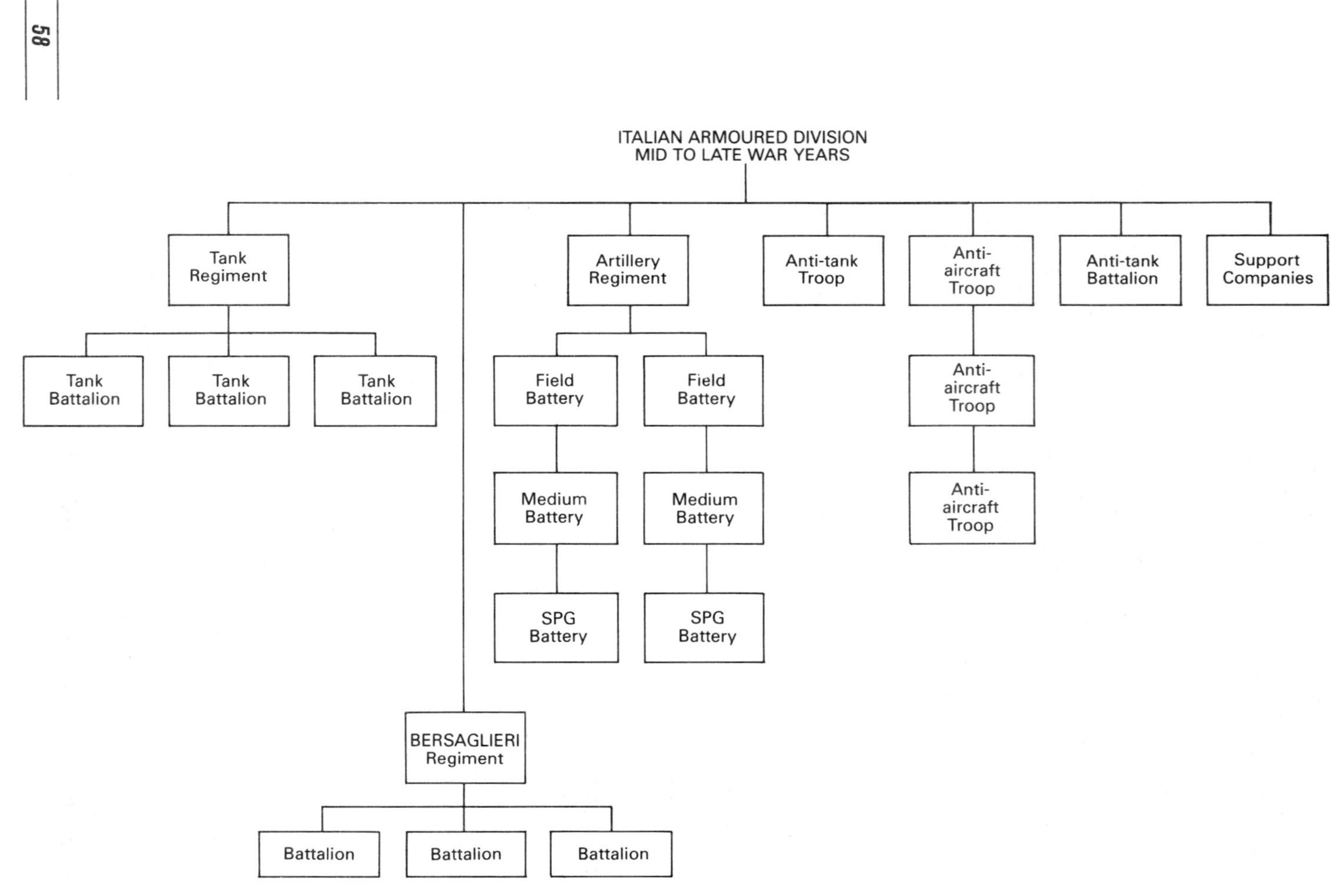

ITALIAN ARMOURED DIVISION
MID TO LATE WAR YEARS
Tank Regiment
Tank Battalion
Tank Battalion
Tank Battalion
Artillery Regiment
Field Battery
Field Battery
Medium Battery
Medium Battery
SPG Battery
SPG Battery
Anti-tank Troop
Anti-aircraft Troop
Anti-aircraft Troop
Anti-aircraft Troop
Anti-tank Battalion
Support Companies
BERSAGLIERI Regiment
Battalion
Battalion
Battalion

four battalions (each 326 men in a headquarters and three parachute companies) and a regiment of artillery with two batteries. At divisional level there were mortar (81 mm), motorcycle and engineer companies.

In Allied Service

In September 1943 the First Motorised Combat Group composed of Italian troops came into being and fought well at Cassino. In April of the following year, this unit became the Italian Liberation Corps. More recruits meant that a number of combat groups were formed in 1945, each having two infantry and one artillery regiment, a mixed engineer battalion, two Carbinieri sections and, with support services, totalled over 9,000 men.

Japan

The Japanese divided their armies into army groups, area armies, divisions (there were no corps) and special mission forces. Much smaller than Western forces, a Japanese army would number between 15,000 and 50,000 men. The 18th army which saw service in the south-west Pacific mustered, in April 1943, three divisions, an independent mixed brigade, four independent artillery companies, two machine gun companies, an independent anti-tank battalion, six field artillery battalions, a like number of searchlight companies and supporting elements.

The Infantry Division

A typical infantry division of late 1941 would have three regiments, an artillery regiment, a cavalry or reconnaissance regiment and an engineer regiment. Amongst the divisional support troops would be found staff, signals, a transport regiment, a poor quality medical unit and up to three field hospital staffs of similar status (the Japanese soldier was expected to either fight or die), a water purification unit, an ordnance unit and lastly a veterinary unit. Later in the war, life became complicated, for the Japanese began to categorise their men as 'A' the strongest, 'B' standard and 'C' special. Not all the divisions were of the same level of troops—a standard 'B' division could for example include class 'A' artillery. Quite often the units themselves were further sub-divided, adding to the complications. In essence, there were four types of Japanese division. Firstly the standard division of 'B' troops, which was the type most frequently encountered and then a strengthened one of 'A' types, with a field or mountain artillery regiment and perhaps a unit of tanks. The third type was as the previous division, but excluding the tank element, and the rifle companies were weaker at 205 men each. Lastly came the special division with two brigades of 'C' troops, each of four independent battalions with 'A' type supporting elements.

Looking at the infantry division in more detail, we find that the divisional commander may have had the use of a tankette company (80–120 men, 10–17 tankettes) for reconnaissance purposes, organised into three or four platoons with a company train. The infantry regiment had a headquarters of 55 officers and men, a train company, signal company, regimental infantry gun train (headquarters of 24 men, one company of two platoons each with two low velocity infantry guns, the other with three platoons, each having two 37mm (later 47mm) anti-tank guns), anti-tank company, possibly some pioneers and three battalions of infantry. Supporting the division and independent of it, would be a three battalion regiment of field or mountain artillery. Each battalion had twelve 75mm guns which could be horsedrawn, motorised or pack transportable. Also included would be three gun companies, each having four 75mm guns, which, with the regimental supply train, brought the manpower total to 2,300. The cavalry regiment had three rifle and sabre companies totalling 950 men.

The Armoured Division

Consisting of three regiments of tanks, a regiment of artillery and a motorised infantry brigade, the Japanese armoured division mustered 3,800 men. The tank regiments each fielded 90 light and medium tanks, organised as a headquarters, three or four tank companies and supported by an ammunition train. The artillery had eight 105 mm guns and four 155 mm howitzers but there was also an anti-tank unit with eighteen 47 mm guns and an anti-aircraft section manning sixteen 20 mm guns. Including supports, the armoured division fielded 10,500 men and 1,850 vehicles.

Independent and Specialised Units

There was a tendency to dissipation in the Japanese army with independent units frequently occurring. Further, the heavier supportive elements—anti-tank and artillery—were retained in their own independent formations, rather than being allocated to any one unit. Raiding forces were used late on in the war and these were usually formed from infantry units. Small—typically headquarters (3 men) with demolition/assault (15), support (12) and reserve (12) sections—but effective, such forces were widely used to carry out raids, attack strong points and so on. Suicide squads also existed who defended a position literally to the death.

Amphibious Brigade

After 1941, some amphibious brigades came into being. Each had three infantry battalions of 1,035 men organised into three rifle

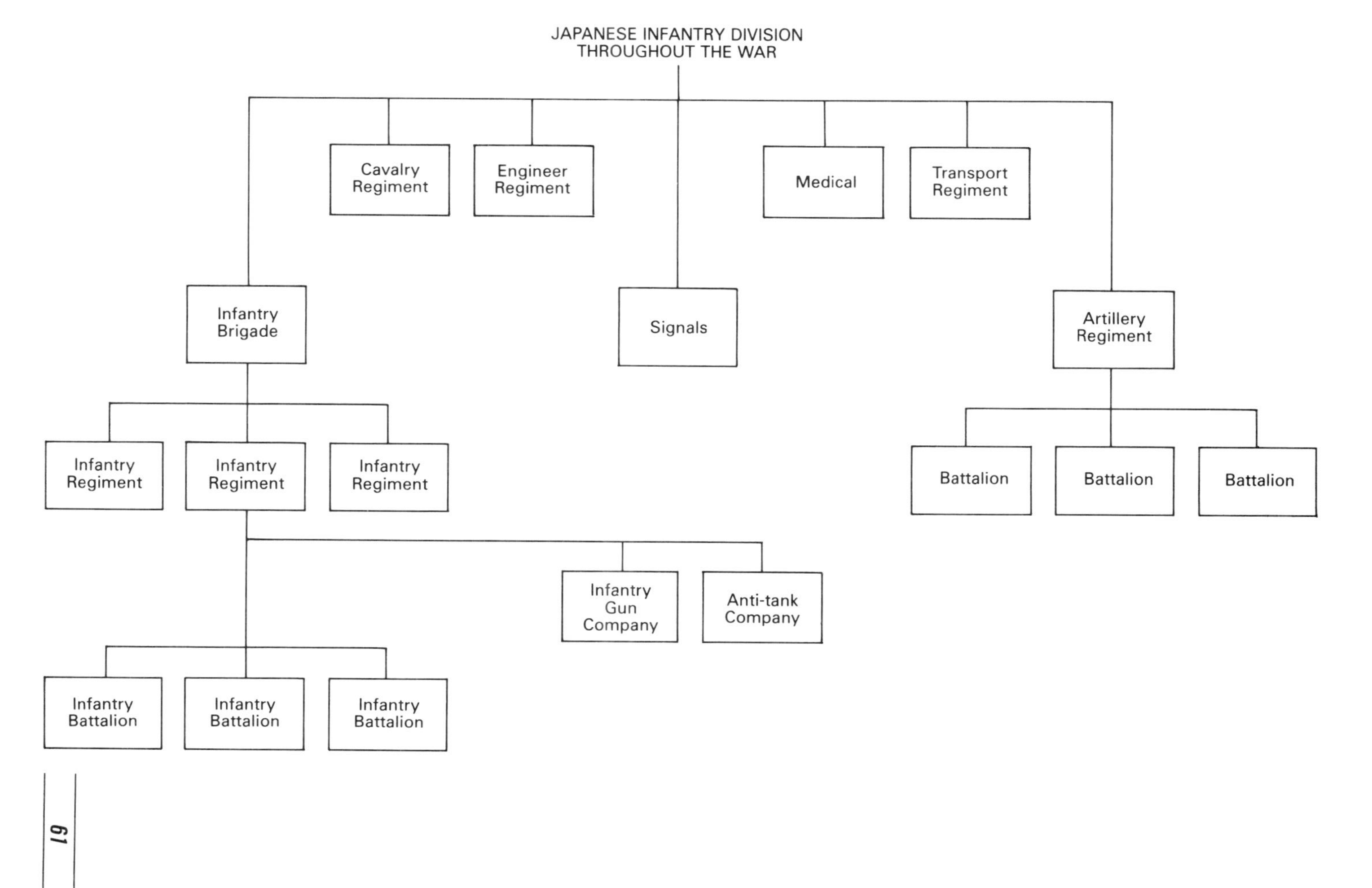

JAPANESE INFANTRY DIVISION
THROUGHOUT THE WAR
Cavalry Regiment
Engineer Regiment
Signals
Medical
Transport Regiment
Artillery Regiment
Infantry Brigade
Infantry Regiment
Infantry Regiment
Infantry Regiment
Infantry Gun Company
Anti-tank Company
Infantry Battalion
Infantry Battalion
Infantry Battalion
Battalion
Battalion
Battalion

A Churchill tank crew operating in Holland.

companies (195 each) sub-divided into three platoons of four sections, supported by a trench mortar platoon. Typically a brigade could be 3,200 men strong and have armour, artillery, engineer, machine gun and signal support.

Japanese Allies

Never very taken with the idea, Japan formed allied units from only two main sources, Burma and India. The Burma Defence army was formed with seven infantry divisions, along with artillery support which was used for mainly garrison duties. Changing its name to the Burma National Army in September 1943 did little to improve the quality and in 1945, the Army defected to the British forces. The India National Army, seeking to remove British rule from India, was raised from Indian prisoners of war in early 1942. By the end of that year, one division was assembled, consisting of three guerilla units, the Azad, Gandhi and Nehru battalions and the three battalion strong No. 1 Hindi Field Force Group. The supportive functions included the customary artillery, engineer, medical, signal and transport. A second division was planned, but the Japanese, due to a general Indian reluctance to fight for them, reduced the first division down to a fraction of its strength. One Subhas Chandra Bose, who had already formed a Free India Legion in Germany, persuaded the Japanese to reconsider and even contemplate a third division. The first division eventually saw a good deal of action in Burma and Malaya during the first six months of 1944, losing 4,400 men.

Naval Land Forces

The naval landing forces were the Japanese version of marines. Initially, they were organised into battalions of four companies and 2,000 strong. The first three companies each had six rifle and one heavy machine gun platoon, whilst the fourth had three rifle platoons and a heavy weapons platoon of four 3" naval guns, two 75 mm regimental guns and two 70 mm battalion guns. The battalions could, on occasion, be supported either by armoured car or tank units. When used to seize the smaller islands, the battalions would field two rifle companies, supported by one or perhaps two heavy weapon companies.

Poland

The Infantry Division

The Polish army had 39 infantry divisions, although this figure did include nine reserve formations. Each division had three infantry regiments and a light or field artillery regiment. Divisional support services included a reconnaissance company equipped with tankettes. Rifle regiments (1,900 men strong) had a headquarters, three battalions, an administrative company, a platoon of pioneers and a signals company. The field artillery regiment was organised into three batteries, each of three troops, each of four guns. Usually the mostly horsedrawn ordnance consisted of twenty-four 75 mm M1897/17 and twelve 100 mm Austrian M14 howitzers. To complete the regimental line up was a headquarters staff and a signals troop. This latter unit was not present in mountain artillery formations, but otherwise these were as their field colleagues, but equipped with 65 mm and 75 mm mountain guns as well as 100 mm howitzers.

At all levels the Polish army was short of artillery both in quality and quantity, with few, if any, units having their full quota of guns.

The Cavalry Brigades

Poland had no less than 11 cavalry brigades, made up from three regiment was divided into two groups, a field gun—forty-two 76 mm and fifty-four 45 mm guns, and a howitzer group with twelve 152 mm and twenty-eight 122 mm weapons. There were also over 100 mortars of varying calibres from 50 mm to 120 mm which could be called on for fire support. As the war progressed the divisions decreased in size, but increased in firepower.

Armoured Formations

Quite simply, there weren't any. It is true that the Poles did have a small tank force—170 light tanks, 50 medium tanks, 67 light tanks of Great War vintage, 700 tankettes and 100 armoured cars (all figures approximate)—but these were never organised as such before being swamped by the Germans in 1939.

In British Service

Towards the end of 1940, a Polish Corps was formed with a strength of over 14,000, organised into two infantry brigades and supplemented by a British medium field artillery regiment. There were no armoured formations within the corps.

An independent Polish Carpathian rifle brigade was raised in the Middle East by the French. Swelled by Poles released from Russian prisoner of war camps, this formation became the 3rd Carpathian Rifle Division in May 1942. Re-equipped and trained by the British, the force became the II Polish Army Corps, arriving in Italy late in 1943.

The Soviet Union

The Infantry

The Russian field army consisted, early in the war, of 100 rifle divisions, including 23 Territorial divisions, organised into 35 corps, 32 cavalry divisions in seven corps, 12 independent cavalry divisions, ten tank brigades in five corps and a motorised rifle brigade. A rifle corps mustered three or four infantry divisions, a regiment of artillery, a bridging battalion, a pioneer battalion, a signals battalion and a squadron of aircraft.

The rifle division was the basic Russian formation, which early in the war had three infantry regiments (2,900 strong) each of three battalions, each battalion having three rifle companies supported by a machine gun and mortar company. The divisional artillery regiment was divided into two groups, a field gun – forty-two mm and fifty-four 45 mm guns, and a howitzer group with twelve 152 mm and twenty-eight 122 mm weapons. There were also over 100 mortars of varying calibres from 50 mm to 120 mm which could be called on for fire support. As the war progressed the divisions decreased in size, but increased in firepower.

By the end of 1942 a division had 9,500 men, organised as three infantry regiments (2,500 each), an artillery regiment, anti-tank and engineer battalions, reconnaissance and signals companies. The rifle regiment still had three battalions now 620 strong and supported by companies of 76 mm howitzers, 45 mm anti-tank guns, anti-tank rifles, mortars and supply elements. Each battalion consisted of three rifle companies still, again with mortar and machine gun companies but also now anti-tank gun, anti-tank rifle and signal platoons. The artillery regiment now had 36 anti-tank rifles, twenty-four 76 mm guns and twelve 122 mm howitzers.

Later Russian armies were organised into groups of two to four corps, each having two to four divisions. The corps formation was found to be unwieldy and was for a time scrapped in favour of the

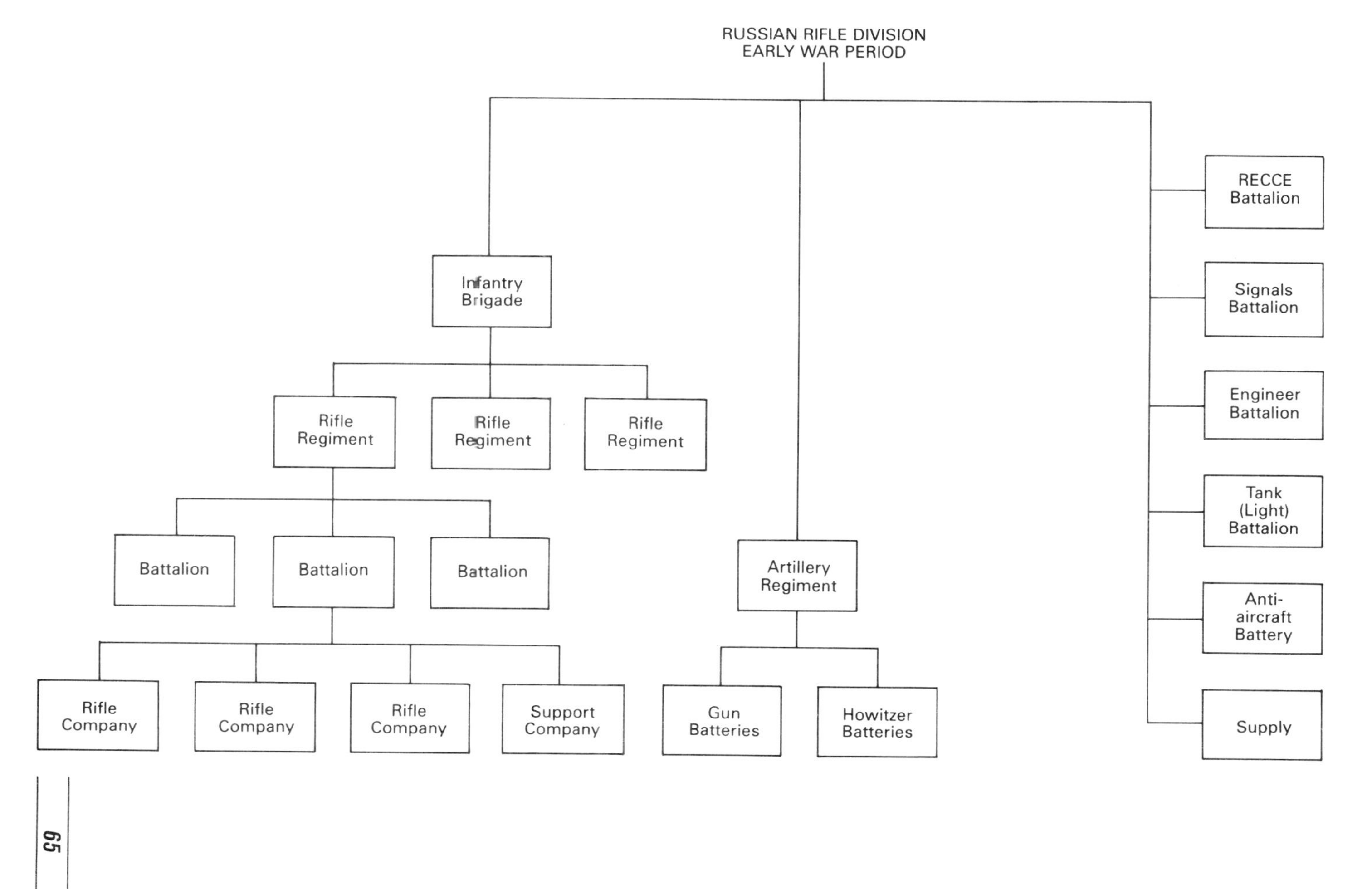

RUSSIAN RIFLE DIVISION
EARLY WAR PERIOD
Infantry Brigade
Rifle Regiment
Rifle Regiment
Rifle Regiment
Battalion
Battalion
Battalion
Rifle Company
Rifle Company
Rifle Company
Support Company
Artillery Regiment
Gun Batteries
Howitzer Batteries
RECCE Battalion
Signals Battalion
Engineer Battalion
Tank (Light) Battalion
Anti-aircraft Battery
Supply

division, an army having typically eight. By 1944 there were no less than 48 Russian infantry armies supported by a varying number of other units.

The Artillery

The Russians placed much reliance on the artillery and experimented with larger and larger groupings, a fact which influenced the German thinking (see above). The artillery was organised into 140 light regiments. Each regiment had a staff, staff battery, anti-aircraft battery and three or four batteries each of three or four guns. In addition, there were 35 corps heavy artillery regiments using tractor-drawn 150 mm guns and howitzers and 20 reserve regiments for use at Supreme Commander level. Later in the war, artillery divisions were created of typically four brigades with fire control and signals units. The four brigades were a mortar brigade (100 anti-tank rifles and 100 120 mm heavy mortars), a light field artillery brigade with three regiments (each twenty-four 76 mm guns), a howitzer brigade (forty-eight 122 mm and twenty-four 152 mm howitzers) and finally a medium field artillery brigade of twelve 122 mm guns and twenty-four 152 mm gun-howitzers.

Mechanised Infantry

The mechanised corps was an important Russian formation which consisted of three brigades of mechanised infantry, a tank brigade and an artillery unit. The mechanised brigade had three battalions (650 each) of motorised infantry with integral support in the shape of 82 mm mortars, 45 mm anti-tank guns, plus anti-tank rifles and so forth. The artillery regiment was self-propelled and divided into four companies each with five 76 mm, 85 mm, 100 mm, 122 mm and 152 mm guns or 85 mm guns. Each brigade had a battalion of 31 or 41 tanks, which, when added to the tank brigade and the self-propelled artillery gave the mechanised corps some 200 plus armoured fighting vehicles.

Armoured Formations

The Russians concentrated their tanks in large formations, centred on either the brigade of three battalions plus reconnaissance battalion and a motorised machine gun battalion or the tank brigade (80–90 tanks) of four battalions. Both of these formations were in addition to the tank battalion allotted to some infantry divisions, those in the mechanised sections of cavalry units and the reserve brigades of heavy tanks. As more and more tanks were produced, they formed independent tank brigades of three battalions, giving 63 tanks overall. These new brigades were supported by a machine gun battalion, anti-aircraft and anti-tank companies. These brigades

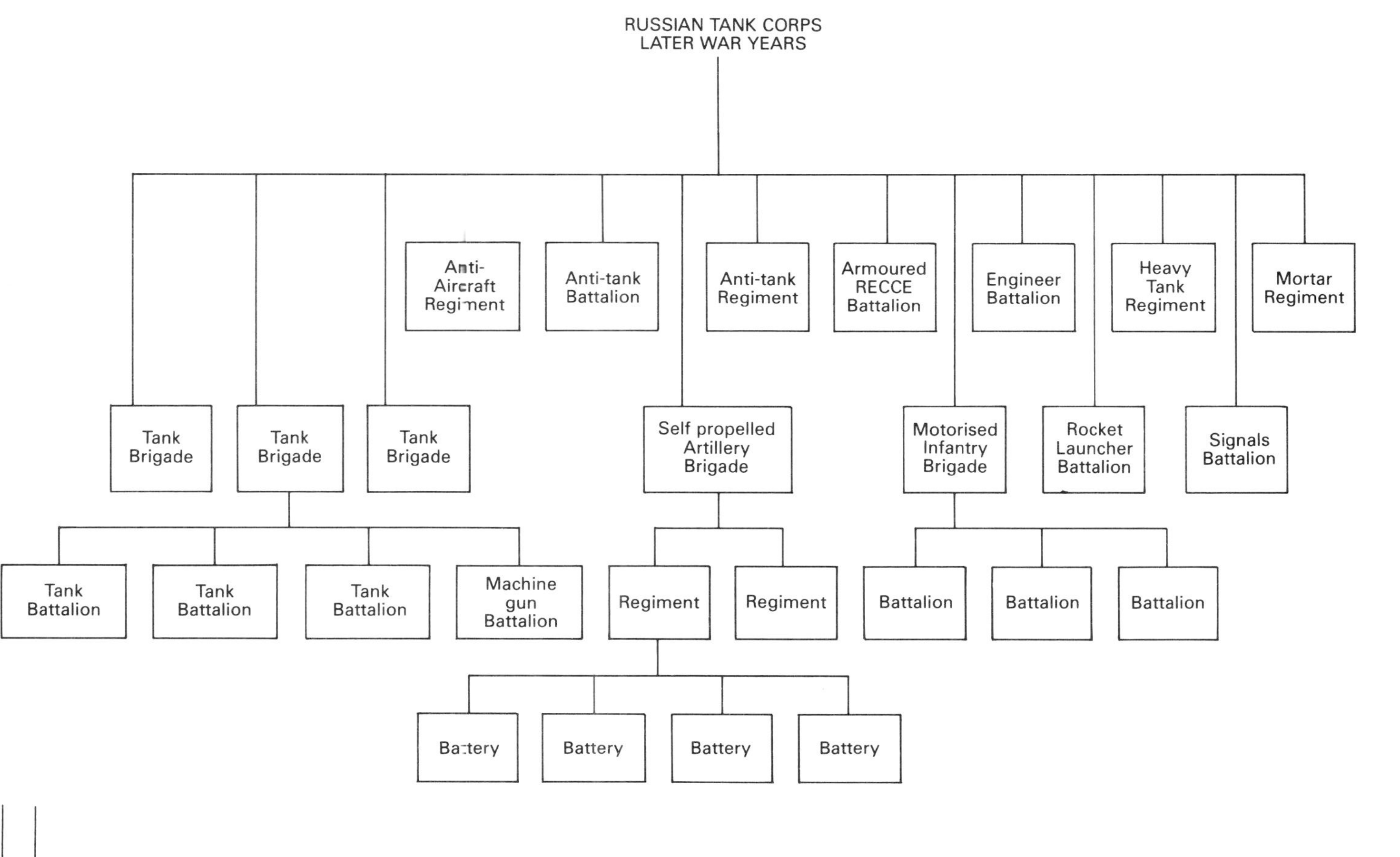

RUSSIAN TANK CORPS
LATER WAR YEARS
Anti-Aircraft Regiment
Anti-tank Battalion
Anti-tank Regiment
Armoured RECCE Battalion
Engineer Battalion
Heavy Tank Regiment
Mortar Regiment
Tank Brigade
Tank Brigade
Tank Brigade
Self propelled Artillery Brigade
Motorised Infantry Brigade
Rocket Launcher Battalion
Signals Battalion
Tank Battalion
Tank Battalion
Tank Battalion
Machine gun Battalion
Regiment
Regiment
Battalion
Battalion
Battalion
Battery
Battery
Battery
Battery

were then combined into tank corps of which there were 26 by 1943. Generally, such corps provided in the region of 200 tanks organised in three brigades, plus a motorised rifle brigade and extensive supporting units, including two regiments of self-propelled artillery (each four batteries of five 85 mm guns). By 1944 there were six tank armies in existence, usually based on two tank corps, together with a mechanised corps.

Cavalry Units

Great trust was placed in the cavalry due to the poor roads and minimal railway network in Russia. A cavalry corps would have a staff, corps troops and three cavalry divisions each of two cavalry brigades of two regiments, two motorised rifle battalions, a horse artillery regiment, an armoured car or tank regiment, a pioneer and signals squadron and a supply unit. The cavalry regiments themselves had a headquarters staff, five squadrons, one cart carried machine gun squadron, a 76 mm equipped horse artillery battery, chemical, pioneer and signals units and lastly a baggage train. There were 40 cavalry divisions in 1941 and by 1945 there were 34. By then, the division (5040 men, 5128 horses, 130 vehicles) had three cavalry regiments, an artillery regiment and supportive units including ten light tanks.

Motorised Anti-tank Brigades

Often used as spearhead troops, the motorised anti-tank brigades were organised as three anti-tank regiments, each of six batteries, each in turn having four 76 mm guns.

United Kingdom

The Infantry Division

As the British army went to war, the basic organisational unit was the infantry division (13,600 strong) which consisted of three brigades of infantry, three regiments of artillery and supporting services. The artillery regiments each had two batteries one of twelve 18 pounders, the other having a like number of 4.5″ howitzers. The anti-tank regiment manned four batteries of twelve 2 pounder guns and there were also three brigade anti-tank companies. The divisional cavalry regiment consisted of 28 light tanks and 44 Universal carriers organised into three squadrons. The infantry brigades each consisted of three battalions (each 813), organised as four rifle companies—each having a headquarters and three platoons—and a headquarters company providing, within its six platoons, administration, anti-aircraft, carrier, pioneer, mortar and signals. In support were medium artillery regiments, composed of two batteries each of eight

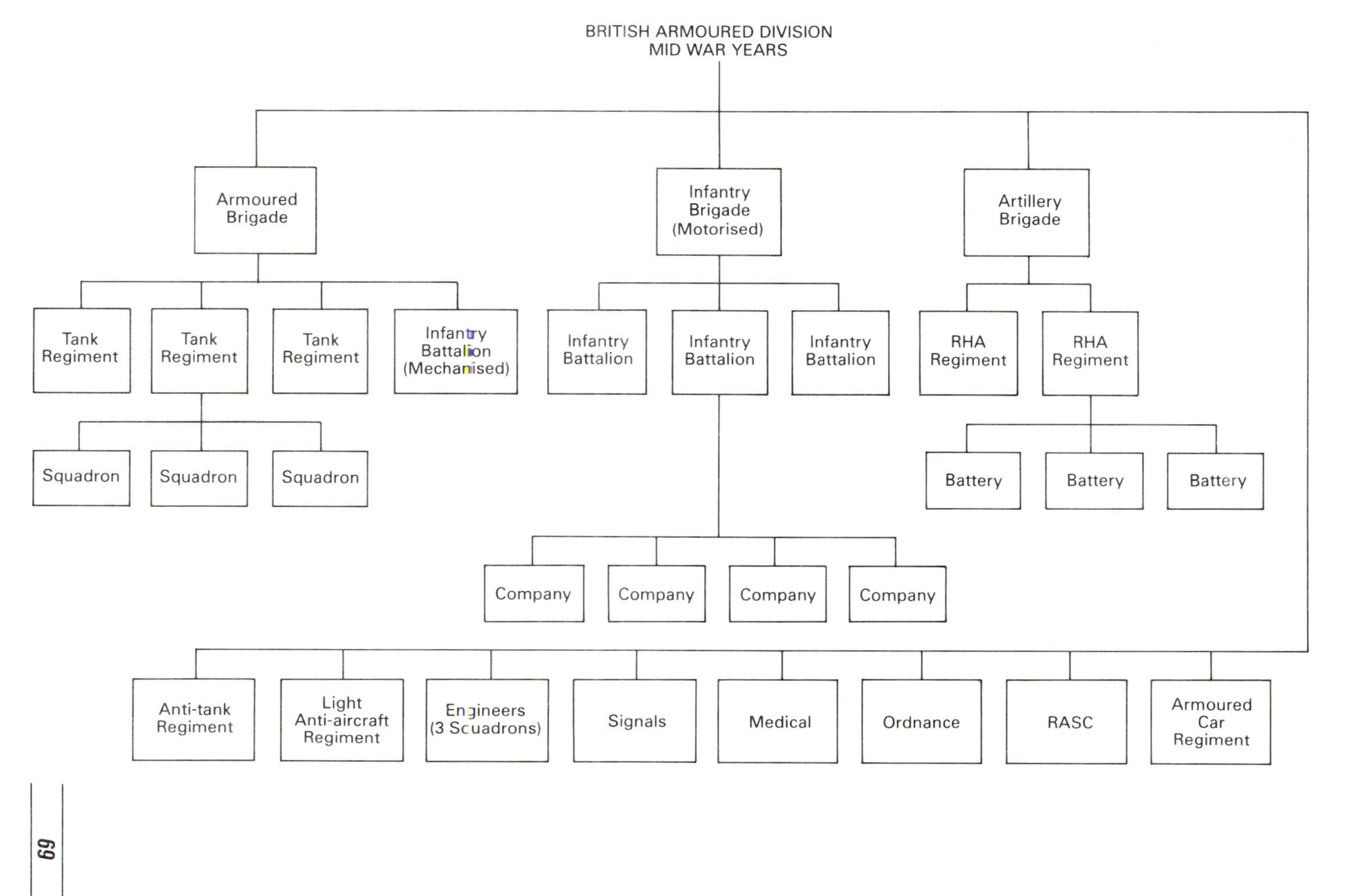

BRITISH ARMOURED DIVISION
MID WAR YEARS
Armoured Brigade
Infantry Brigade (Motorised)
Artillery Brigade
Tank Regiment
Tank Regiment
Tank Regiment
Infantry Battalion (Mechanised)
Squadron
Squadron
Squadron
Infantry Battalion
Infantry Battalion
Infantry Battalion
Company
Company
Company
Company
RHA Regiment
RHA Regiment
Battery
Battery
Battery
Anti-tank Regiment
Light Anti-aircraft Regiment
Engineers (3 Squadrons)
Signals
Medical
Ordnance
RASC
Armoured Car Regiment

pieces—6" howitzers or 60 pounders—and heavy regiments with four 4 gun batteries, one of 6" howitzers and three of 9.2" howitzers.

Armoured Formations

Initially, the British armoured brigade had three armoured regiments, each having a headquarters and three tank squadrons, providing 52 tanks. The largest tank formation was the armoured division which, early in the war, consisted of two armoured brigades, an artillery support group and two motorised infantry battalions. Later, (1942–43) the armoured division increased radically in size and firepower. The armoured brigade—three armoured regiments, each 61 tanks, and a mechanised infantry battalion—provided nearly 200 tanks, whilst the artillery mustered forty-eight 25 pounder guns. The motorised infantry brigade still had three battalions, each of four companies and an armoured car regiment of four squadrons was added, giving the division 60 armoured cars.

To a greater degree than perhaps any other nation, Great Britain altered or amended her organisations to suit localised needs. The constantly changing divisions in North Africa, for example, bore little relation to those in the United Kingdom. To record those changes would be tedious in the extreme and would exhaust the reader's patience as surely as it would the author's knowledge. Suffice to say then, that the varying commanders often reorganised the frequently meagre forces at their disposal to meet their immediate needs or to suit their intended plans.

United States

The Infantry Division

When the United States entered the war, the infantry division had three infantry regiments, an artillery regiment of 48 howitzers and supporting units. This basic organisation continued in use in fact throughout the rest of the war and by 1944 mustered 14,253 men. The 1944 infantry regiment had a headquarters company, an infantry gun company, equipped with six 105 mm infantry howitzers, an anti-tank company with twelve 57 mm pieces, a service company, all supporting three infantry battalions of 860 men each. The artillery regiment attached mustered one battalion of medium artillery (three batteries each of four 155 mm howitzers) and three of light artillery, similarly organised, but with 105 mm howitzers.

The Armoured Division

The early armoured divisions comprised a reconnaissance battalion and four tank battalions. By 1942 this had grown to field 159 medium

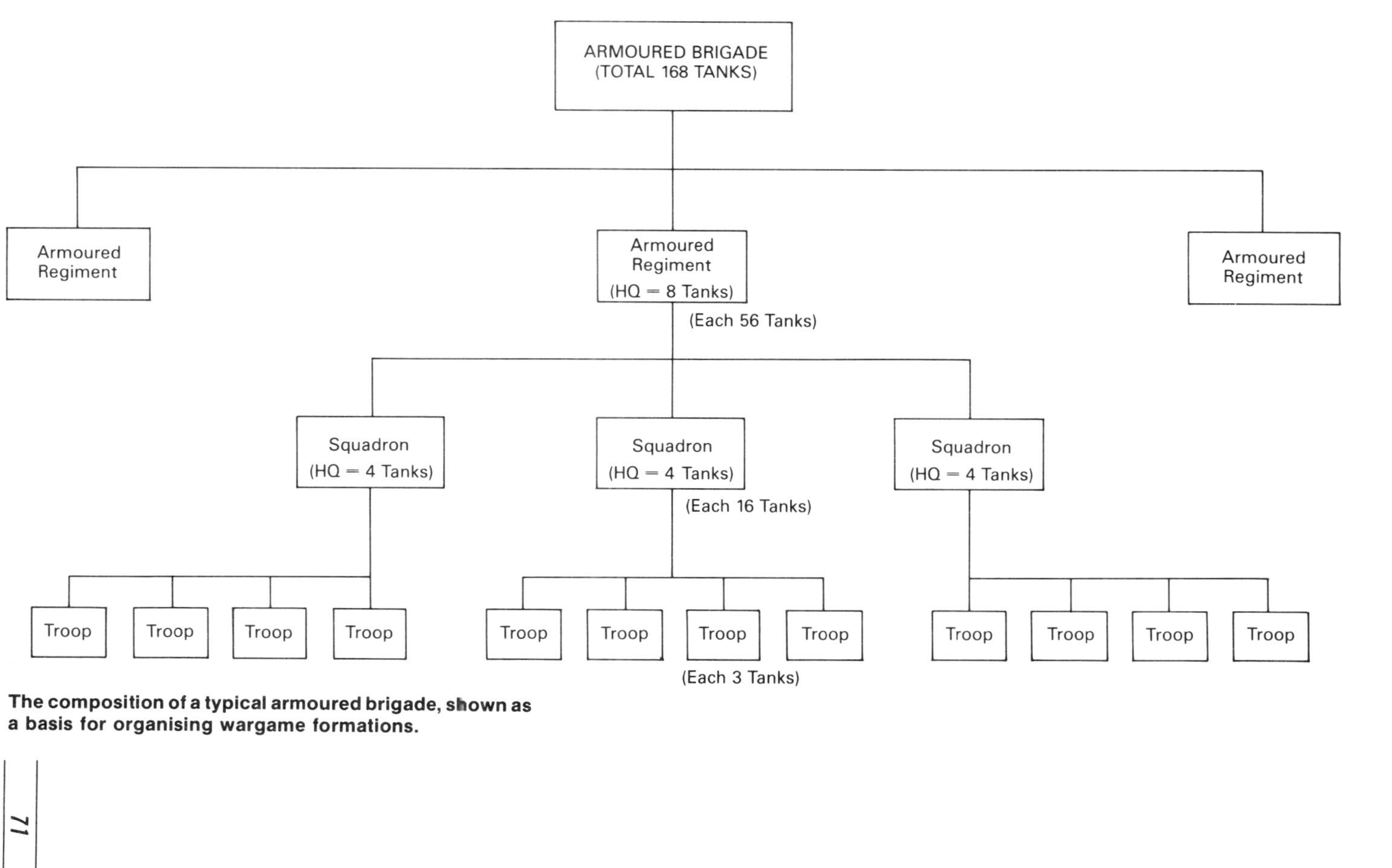

The composition of a typical armoured brigade, shown as a basis for organising wargame formations.

and 68 light tanks, supported by an armoured and motorised three battalion strong infantry regiment. The artillery component consisted of three battalions each equipped with 18 self-propelled 105 mm howitzers and the division mustered 10,900 men overall. In the same year, the armoured division was reorganised as two Combat Commands, each one battalion of artillery, infantry and tanks. Since this system provided for highly mobile forces, by late 1943 it was standard, but with three Combat Commands per division. By 1944 the armoured division featured an engineer battalion, a reconnaissance squadron of five troops, signals company, three tank battalions (each three medium tank companies of 18 tanks and one of 17 light tanks), three armoured infantry battalions (each three rifle companies) and finally three field artillery battalions each three batteries of six 105 mm self-propelled howitzers.

Tank Battalions

In addition to the armoured divisions, a number of semi-independent tank battalions were formed. These 68 tank strong battalions were organised in much the same manner as the divisional tank battalions—one light and three medium tank companies. Whilst they often worked alone, the tank battalions could be deployed in groups of three or five and as such, when grouped with armoured infantry formations, were termed armoured groups.

Of a similar nature were the highly mobile tank destroyer battalions, each consisting of 36 self propelled anti-tank guns.

Airborne Forces

In 1941 only one parachute battalion was in existence, but the war years saw a rapid expansion in this area. By 1944 there were two divisions of paratroopers, with two more forming. The airborne division had one parachute regiment and two glider-borne infantry regiments, totalling, with supports, 8,505 men. By September 1944 the divisions had 12,979 men having been reorganised and mustering as follows: two parachute regiments, each 2364 men in three battalions, one glider-borne infantry regiment of 2978 in three battalions with a regimental headquarters, service company, anti-tank company, anti-aircraft/anti-tank battalion of three machine gun batteries (each of 12 machine guns) and three gun batteries (each eight 57 mm anti-tank guns) and three batteries of divisional artillery with 75 mm pack howitzers.

The Marine Corps

In February 1941 the Marine Corps had an establishment of two brigades, each of which was expanded into a division by mid 1942.

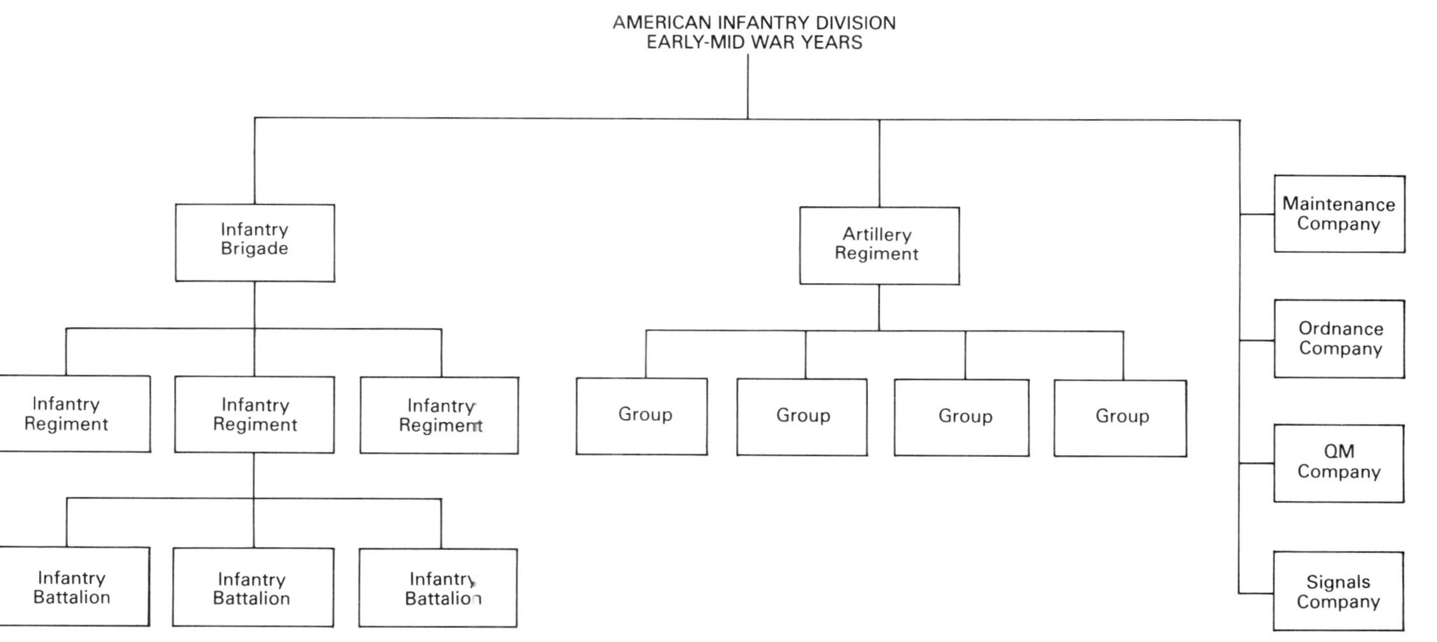

AMERICAN INFANTRY DIVISION
EARLY-MID WAR YEARS
Infantry Brigade
Artillery Regiment
Maintenance Company
Ordnance Company
QM Company
Signals Company
Infantry Regiment
Infantry Regiment
Infantry Regiment
Group
Group
Group
Group
Infantry Battalion
Infantry Battalion
Infantry Battalion

Each division had three infantry regiments, each of three battalions, along with artillery, engineer and pioneer regiments. These two divisions were combined into the First Marine Amphibious Corps and during 1943, three more divisions were raised, followed by another the following year. A new corps was formed in 1943 and the First was re-titled III Amphibious Corps.

Organising Wargames Armies

In the previous section, we looked at the internal organisation of the various formations of the major combatant nations during the war, and we now need to use this information to organise our wargame forces. It is difficult, not to say impossible, to recreate large formations on a one-to-one basis in miniature, even in 1/300th scale and, as a result, some form of rationalisation or scaling down will be necessary. Let us look at a couple of examples, taking, say, a British Armoured Division of the 1942–43 period as a model.

Although the organisation tended to vary somewhat, it is fairly safe to say that the armoured brigade within the Division had a headquarters staff or unit which fielded ten tanks and three armoured regiments, each of which had between 40 and 60 tanks, so some 130 to 190 tanks in total. The regiments for their part were composed of a headquarters and three squadrons, with each squadron having a headquarters and four troops. There were three tanks in a troop, which, along with the four tanks allocated to squadron headquarters gave a squadron an average strength each of some 16 tanks. Carrying this a little further, we see that if the squadrons mustered 16 tanks, then the regiment, along with its headquarters of eight tanks, could muster in the region of 56. It must be stressed that, while serving our purposes as an example here, this must only be regarded as an average figure, for the establishments of units did vary considerably, not only from the 'norm', but from one formation to another. To field the 56 tanks of the armoured regiment in a wargame would indeed be awkward, whereas over three times this number—in other words the brigade—would just not be on.

So, what can we do? There are 12 troops in a regiment—if we allow one wargames tank to represent a troop, then we shall need 36 for the brigade, which offers a small saving. If, however, we let one miniature tank stand for a squadron, only three would be needed for each regiment and a total of nine for the entire brigade. Representing as it does a considerable saving in vehicles, this method may not be aesthetically pleasing to everyone, although it is one worth examining for potential. Such a system provides a roughly 1:16 ratio which should then, for the sake of uniformity, be applied to the other formations within the armoured division. The divisional RHA brigade of forty-eight 25 pdr guns would then be de-

A Vickers Mark VI tank comes to grief in France 1940.

This picture taken from German sources shows a disabled Matilda Mark 1 infantry tank of the 7th Royal Tank Regiment.

picted by three models, each representing two batteries which is not terribly convenient, but tolerable enough perhaps. The 16 companies of the motorised infantry brigade would clearly be represented by one, whilst the armoured car regiment would be allotted three or four vehicles. This will all work out, but the armoured division is a large formation and some wargamers may prefer to field just a tank squadron or an infantry company and use a 1:5 or 1:10 ratio. Split into three platoons—each of three sections of typically ten men—and a headquarters, the infantry company can even be portrayed on a 1:1 ratio. This would imply an 'infantry only' action however, for on this basis, armoured accompaniment would be tricky to scale in.

Much will depend on the size of the wargames material in use—what looks good in 25 mm may well look silly in 1/300th scale and the reverse is equally true. It may be possible—just—to field over 50 tanks per side in 1/300 and still manage some sort of action, but in 25 mm there simply will not be room on the table. Similarly, an interesting infantry action in 25mm set at company or platoon level will be relatively boring and certainly lacking in visual interest when conducted with 1/300th scale soldiers. Many World War II wargamers have figures and vehicles in more than one scale—the relatively new 1/200 size items in particular are creating a great deal of interest—and simply use the items most suitable for the particular action to hand. It is equally satisfying to carry out a reconnaissance patrol in the Burmese jungle as to thunder across the Russian steppes with one's Panzer divisions.

For these reasons, there is little argument in favour of a total uniformity in scale across the wargamer's miniature forces. This

This photograph of a Tiger I tank is taken from the German "Signal" magazine.

must be unique to World War II, since this is a prime requisite in other periods, but perhaps it serves to reflect the huge and differing nature of the conflict.

Weaponry

Numerous references have already been made to a variety of weapons. In this section, these weapons will be looked at in more detail. It is always difficult in such a summary to decide what information to include and what to omit. A great deal will depend on the rules which the individual wargamer uses for his or her World War Two games. Some rules may call for accurate records of petrol consumption to be kept, whilst others are more concerned with the expenditure of ammunition. In an armoured engagement, the performance details of a hand-held pistol could be viewed as somewhat inconsequential, while the performance of a V2 rocket is pretty irrelevant within the context of an infantry action.

One of the most difficult items to summate meaningfully is probably that of the defensive armour on a tank. The thickness varied on different parts of all armoured vehicles and from mark to mark of a particular model. Frequently the normal or stated protection was 'locally' improved by tank crews bolting lengths of track or spare wheels onto the hull. My adopted policy on this aspect, therefore, is to include such details where relevant in order that the wargamer can gain some sort of comparison in armour thickness between the various tanks which will be listed.

In order to facilitate easier cross-reference, the weapons will be dealt with in largely the same order of countries as the organisational charts above. Some changes however, have been made in the countries covered in this section. The Commonwealth countries were, for the most part, equipped by Britain or America. Only the weapons native to those countries will be covered under their respective sections; the rest will be dealt with in the supplier's section. Further, the inclusion of Czechslovakia and Poland is necessary in this section of the book, for they eventually provided an important source of vehicles for the Germans. The text is further divided into three sections for each of these nations under the headings Armoured Vehicles, Artillery and Infantry weapons. In the artillery section, any quoted ranges are expressed in metres, unless otherwise stated. With regard to the ranges of the hand-held i.e. infantry weapons, any quoted ranges, with the exception of those for anti-tank weapons and mortars, have not been recorded here. This is because the given ranges are frequently nullified by terrain and the often necessarily low profile of their user—it is all very well to have a rifle which is capable of firing at 2,000 yards when its firer cannot see beyond say 200. One can generalise for wargame purposes and say that a rifle has an effective range of 800 yards, a sub-machine gun 150, a light machine gun 1,000 and a medium or heavy machine gun 1,500 yards. Anti-tank weapons and mortars have been excluded from this stricture, for they are generally regarded in wargames as being akin to the artillery.

Australia

ARMOURED VEHICLES

Tanks
Australia relied on British and American tanks throughout the war, although limited numbers of her own home produced tank, the Sentinel, were manufactured along with a number of variants.

Soviet infantry advance behind KV1 heavy tanks in 1942.

Sentinel Cruiser Tank
Crew: Five
Armament: One 2 pdr gun, two .303 Vickers mgs.
Armour: Maximum 65 mm, minimum 25 mm
Maximum speed: 20 mph
Combat radius: 100 miles
Ammunition stowage: 130 rounds 2 pdr, 4,250 rounds mg.

Grant ARV MKII Unique to the Australian forces, the standard Grant medium tank was converted to an ARV by the removal of its guns and the addition of a spade, tool boxes and a winch.

ARTILLERY

In 1943, the Australians lightened and shortened the 25 pounder gun to facilitate its use in the jungle. The range was as a result, reduced, but still covered 10,000 yards, which was sufficient in the jungle environment.

INFANTRY WEAPONS

As with the vehicles, the bulk of the Australian weaponry was supplied by the Allies, but it is worth noting perhaps, that Australia developed her own 9 mm Austen and Owen smgs, based on Allied patterns.

Canada

ARMOURED VEHICLES

Tanks

Grizzly Cruiser Tank I Based on the design of the M4A1 medium tank, the Grizzly was built in Canada after the Ram series (see below)

A Russian T-26 tank in Persia, in an interesting camouflage.

during the last four months of 1943. Once the decision was made to concentrate the production of the M4 series within the USA, production ceased. The Grizzly however was made in sufficient numbers to equip Canadian armoured formations at home and in Europe. Technical details are as for the M4A1, covered in the US section, apart from the fact that 78 rounds of 75 mm ammunition were carried.

Skink Anti-Aircraft Tank To meet the demand for an anti-aircraft tank in preparation for Operation *Overlord*, the Grizzly was fitted with a modified turret to take four 20 mm cannons. In the event, few Skinks came into production, due to the Allies gaining air superiority and thus largely removing the need for specialised anti-aircraft armoured vehicles.

Ram Cruiser Tank, Mkl or ll Based on the American M3 chassis, Canada's own tank came into service in 1942 as the Mk I Ram, armed with a 2 pdr gun. The later Mk II had a 6 pdr gun, but it was not as a result of its firepower that the Ram saw action. The numerous conversions on the basic Ram (in all, some 12 variants were produced) provided the Allied forces with a supply of specialised armoured vehicles—notably the Kangaroo APC, the first to be used by the British army. The US classification for the Ram was M4A5.
Crew: Five
Armament: 2 pdr (Mk I), 6 pdr (Mk II) two .30 Browning mgs, one .30 Browning mg in an anti-aircraft role.
Armour: Maximum 87 mm, minimum 57 mm
Maximum speed: 20 mph
Combat radius: 144 miles
Ammunition stowage: 171 rounds 2 pdr (Mk I), 92 rounds 6 pdr (Mk II) and 4,400 mg rounds.

ARTILLERY

Self-propelled artillery A number of self-propelled guns supplied by the Allies were used by the Canadians, and these will be covered in the sections dealing with the particular country, but one home produced weapon is dealt with here.

Sexton Self-propelled Gun Based on the Ram chassis, the Sexton provided a mobile platform for the 25 pdr gun. Similar to the American M7 Priest (see below), but with the 105 mm gun removed, the gun came into service with the field artillery regiments of armoured divisions in 1943.
Crew: Six

Early Stug III variant German self-propelled gun, disabled by the British in Tunisia, late 1942.

Armament: 25 pdr gun Mk 2C
Armour: Maximum 108 mm, minimum 12 mm
Maximum speed: 24 mph
Combat radius: 125 miles
Ammunition stowage: 112 rounds.

Czechoslovakia

Early in 1939 Czechoslovakia was annexed by Germany and her entire tank force taken over by the German army. When war was declared, there were only a very limited number of German PzKpfw III and IVs (see below) and the Czech tanks, now designated PzKpfw 38(t) and 35(t), were the most numerous types in service.

ARMOURED VEHICLES

Tanks

Light Tank LT vz 34 (CKD/PRAGA P-II)
Crew: Four
Armament: One 37 mm gun, two 7.92 mm mgs
Armour: Maximum 25 mm, minimum 8 mm
Maximum speed, cross-country: 20 mph
Combat radius: 110 km
Ammunition stowage: 37 mm 50 rounds, 1,800 mg

Light Tank LT vz 38 (CKD PRAGA TNHP) The standard light tank of the Czech army, production continued until 1942 under German control during which time the tank was designated PzKpfw 38(t).
Crew: Three or four
Armament: One 37 mm gun, two 7.92 mm mgs
Armour: Maximum 25 mm, minimum 8 mm
Maximum speed, cross-country: 26 mph

Combat radius: 230 km
Ammunition stowage: 37 mm 90 rounds, 2,400 mg

Medium Tank ST vz 39 (CKD Praga V-8-H)
Crew: Four
Armament: One 47 mm gun, two 7.92 mm mgs
Armour: Maximum 32 mm, minimum 20 mm
Maximum speed, cross-country: 28 mph
Combat radius: 150 km
Ammunition stowage: Gun 90 rounds, 3,000 mg

ARTILLERY

Self-Propelled artillery

S3 Light Self-Propelled Gun
Crew: Five
Armament: One 37.2 mm gun, two 7.92 mm mgs
Armour: Maximum 12 mm
Maximum speed, cross-country: 25 mph
Combat radius: 120 miles

Towed Artillery

Anti-tank artillery
37 mm vz 34 maximum range 5,000
37 mm vz 37 maximum range 5,000
47 mm vz 36 could penetrate 51 mm of armour at 760 yards

Field artillery
10 cm Field Howitzer vz 14/19 maximum range 9,800
8 cm Field Gun vz 30 maximum range 13,500

German infantry, armed with MG42 and MP44 assault rifles, cross in front of a Panther tank.

Heavy artillery
15 cm Howitzer vz 37 maximum range 15,100

Anti-aircraft artillery
4.7 cm vz 37 maximum range 7,100
7.5 cm Kan PP Let vz 32 maximum range 9,750

INFANTRY WEAPONS

The bulk of Czechoslovak infantry weapons were supplied by France and were of French origin.

France

ARMOURED VEHICLES

Tanks

The war record of the French tank ends at 1940, for the Germans appropriated all of them with the fall of France. A number saw service under their conqueror's colours however and some were still in use at the end of the war.

Char B1 bis Heavy Tank At the outbreak of the war, the French main battle tank, the Char B1 bis, was considered to be one of the heaviest and most powerful tanks in service. The tank's 75 mm gun was hull mounted, which meant that the vehicle was virtually a self-propelled gun, even allowing for the 47 mm gun in the turret.
Crew: Four
Armament: one 75 mm gun, one 47 mm gun, two 7.5 mm mgs
Armour: Maximum 60 mm, minimum 20 mm
Maximum speed, cross-country: 17 mph
Combat radius: 93 miles

Renault FT-17 Light Tank
Crew: Two
Armament: One 37 mm gun (or one 8 mm mg)
Armour: Maximum 22 mm, minimum 6 mm
Maximum speed, cross-country: 5 mph
Combat radius: 22 miles

Renault R-35 Light Tank The most numerous light tank in the French army, there were approximately 2,000 in service at the outbreak of war. Many saw service in Russia with the Germans and as late as 1944, were fitted with 47 mm guns and used as anti-tank weapons.
Crew: Two
Armament: One 37 mm gun, one 7.5 mm mg

A Japanese Type 97 tank.

Armour: Maximum 45 mm, minimum 6 mm
Maximum speed, cross-country: 12 mph
Combat radius: 87 miles

Char D2 Medium Tank
Crew: Three
Armament: One 47 mm gun, two 8 mm mgs
Armour: Maximum 40 mm, minimum 6 mm
Maximum speed: 13 mph
Combat radius: 80 miles

Somua S-35 Medium Tank The standard medium tank of the French army and arguably the best French tank of the war.
Crew: Three
Armament: One 47 mm gun, one 7.5 mm mg
Armour: Maximum 55 mm
Maximum speed: 23 mph
Combat radius: 80 miles

Hotchkiss H-35 and H-39 Light Tanks
Crew: Two
Armament: One 37 mm gun, one 7.5 mm mg
Armour: Maximum 40 mm, minimum 12 mm
Maximum speed: 23 mph
Combat radius: 93 miles

ARTILLERY

Towed artillery

Anti-tank artillery
25 mm Hotchkiss Mle 34 maximum range 1,750

Field artillery
75 mm Gun Mle 1897 maximum range 6,850
105 mm Gun Mle 13TR maximum range 12,700

Heavy artillery
155 mm Howitzer Mle 1917 maximum range 11,500
155 mm Gun Mle 17 GPF maximum range 16,200
Canon de 155 L Modele 1932 Schneider maximum range 30,000

INFANTRY WEAPONS

Rifle: Gras & Lebel 8 mm, Mas 7.5 mm
Sub-machine gun (smg): Mas38 7.65 mm
Light machine gun (lmg): Fusil Mitrailleur Modele 1924
Chatellerauit 7.5 mm
Mortar: 81 mm Brandt, 2.9 lb bomb, 2,000 yards

Germany

Probably more information is available on the tanks of Germany than those of any other country. Basically, the German 'family' of tanks was designated as follows; I light training, II light reconnaissance, III medium, IV support, V heavy. The various marks of tanks, as well as the successive types, are well recorded and the wargamer has a wealth of information on which to draw. Since the available space does not permit a fully detailed analysis of all the variants, a selection of the major types is presented here. Those wargamers wishing to add further models to their miniature armies are referred to the bibliography for further reading.

ARMOURED VEHICLES

Tanks

Panzerkampfwagen (PzKpfw) I Ausf A (Std Kfz 101) Light Tank A pre-war tank, used largely for training purposes, but still in service during the early years of the war.
Crew: Two
Armament: Two 7.92 mm mgs
Armour: Maximum 13 mm, minimum 7 mm
Maximum speed: 23 mph
Combat radius: 125 miles
Ammunition stowage: 1,525 rounds

PzKpfw II Light Reconnaissance Tank In 1939 and 1940, the PzKpfw II was the principal tank of the German armoured formations. Many improvements were made, mainly to engine performance and

An M4 Sherman tank in Berlin, 1945.

armour protection. The tank was still in service in 1942, although not with front line units.

Ausf D and E
Crew: Three
Armament: One 2 cm KwK 38 automatic gun, one 7.92 mm mg
Armour: Maximum 30 mm, minimum 10 mm
Maximum speed: 34 mph
Combat radius: 124 miles
Ammunition stowage: 180 rounds 20 mm, 1,425 mg

PzKpfw III Medium Tank Based on the experience gained from the production of the PzKpfw I and II, the PzKpfw III was specifically designed for the German armoured formations as anti-tank, as opposed to a support tank. Several marks were produced and over 4,000 were built.

Ausf B
Crew: Five
Armament: One 3.7 cm KwK, three 7.92 mm mgs
Armour: Maximum 18 mm, minimum 14 mm
Maximum speed: 19 mph
Combat radius: 93 miles
Ammunition stowage: 3.7 cm 150 rounds, 4,500 mg

In summary, the major details of some other versions;

Ausf H
Crew: Five
Armament: 5 cm gun, two mgs
Armour: Maximum 30 mm, minimum 18 mm
Maximum speed: 25 mph

Ausf J As above, but with 18–50 mm armour and a longer L/60 gun on later vehicles.

German infantry follow a PzKpfw IV.

Ausf M Similar to above, but with optional skirt armour.

Ausf N Identical to the Ausf M, apart from being fitted with a short 7.5 cm gun instead of 5 cm, to act as a close support tank.

PzKpfw IV Medium Support Tank The second purpose-built German tank, the PzKpfw IV became the standard tank of the German army. The only German tank in continuous production throughout the war and numerically the most important with over 9,000 being built. Once again, the IV was continually improved, this time in the areas of armour and armament. A long-barrelled 75 mm gun was fitted to the Ausf F and Ausf G versions and equipped with this gun, the PzKpfw IVs were able to take over the anti-tank role from the PzKpfw IIIs. The F2 was used with considerable success by the Afrika Korps in the Western Desert. The Ausf J was the final production model.

Ausf F2-J
Crew: Five
Armament: One 7.5 cm KwK 40 (L/43) gun, two 7.92 mm mgs
Armour: Maximum 50 mm, minimum 10 mm
Maximum speed: 25 mph
Combat radius: 130 miles
Ammunition stowage: 7.5 cm 87 rounds, 3,150 mg

PzKpfw Neubaufahrzeuge V Heavy Tank Used in the Norway campaign in 1940, this heavy tank was scrapped in the following year and its designation passed to the Panther.
Crew: Six

Armament: One 7.5 cm and one 37 mm gun and three mgs (Model
A). One 10.5 cm gun, one 37 mm gun and three mgs (Model B).
Armour: Maximum 70 mm, minimum 10 mm
Maximum speed: 22 mph

PzKpfw V Panther Thought by many observers to be the best German
tank of the war.

Ausf D2 (First production type)
Crew: Four
Armament: One 7.5 cm gun and two mgs
Armour: Maximum 80 mm, minimum 15 mm
Maximum speed: 28 mph
Ammunition stowage: 7.5 cm 79 rounds, 4,104 mg

Ausf G (1944 production model)
Crew: Four
Armament: One 7.5 cm gun and two mgs
Armour: Maximum 120 mm, minimum 15 mm
Maximum speed: 28 mph
Ammunition stowage: 7.5 cm 82 rounds, 4,200 mg

PzKpfw VI Tiger Heavy Tank At the time of its introduction in 1942—and
for a number of years after that date, the Tiger was the most
formidable and the heaviest tank in service.

Ausf E
Crew: Five
Armament: One 8.8 cm L/56 gun, two 7.92 mm mgs
Armour: Maximum 110 mm, minimum 26 mm
Maximum speed: 24 mph
Combat radius: 60 miles
Ammunition stowage: 8.8 cm 92 rounds, 3,920 mg

PzKpfw VI King Tiger II Main Battle Tank Whilst strong on gun calibre and
armour protection, the King Tiger was dogged by poor performance
and engine failure, due largely to the engine being over-stressed by
the weight of the vehicle. This fact aside, the Tiger II proved
extremely difficult to 'kill', but fortunately for the Allies, less than 500
came into service between its arrival in November 1944 and the end
of the war.
Crew: Five
Armament: One 8.8 cm L/71 gun, two 7.92 mm mgs
Armour: Maximum 185 mm, minimum 40 mm
Maximum speed: 21 mph

Combat radius: 105 miles
Ammunition stowage: 8.8 cm 84 rounds, 5,850 mg

Tank Destroyers

Elefant Heavy Tank Destroyer   There were, at the initial design stage of the Tiger, two versions, Henschel and Porsche. When the former was selected, the Porsche chassis were used for heavy tank destroyers. In all 90 Elefants were built and the first entered service in July 1943 at Kirsk. Due to their total lack of any secondary armament, by the end of 1944, none remained in service.
remained in service.
Crew: Six
Armament: 8.8 cm PAK 43 anti-tank gun
Armour: Maximum 200 mm, minimum 30 mm
Maximum speed: 12 mph
Combat radius: 95 miles
Ammunition stowage: Unknown

Hertzer Tank Destroyer A most successful vehicle, over 2,500 Hertzers were built and many remained in use with various armies after the war.
Crew: Four
Armament: One 7.5 cm PAK 39 gun
Armour: Maximum 60 mm, minimum 8 mm
Maximum speed: 26 mph
Combat radius: 108 miles
Ammunition stowage: 41 rounds

Jagdpanther Tank Destroyer The Jagdpanther utilised the Panther hull and provided an anti-tank platform for the 8.8 cm gun.
Crew: Five
Armament: 8.8 cm PAK 43/3 gun
Armour: Maximum 80 mm, minimum 15 mm
Maximum speed: 29 mph
Combat radius: 100 miles
Ammunition stowage: 57 rounds

Jagdpanzer IV Tank Destroyer Intended to replace the Sturmgeschutze III, the Jagdpanzer IV was an efficient weapon which featured a newly designed hull.
Crew: Four
Armament: One 7.5 cm PAK 40 gun
Armour: Maximum 80 mm, minimum 10 mm
Maximum speed: 25 mph

Two knocked out French Char B1 bis tanks in France, 1940.

Combat radius: 130 miles
Ammunition stowage: 79 rounds

Jagdtiger Tank Destroyer Following the usual German practice of placing heavy guns in existing tank chassis, the Jagdtiger utilised the Tiger II hull.
Crew: Six
Armament: One 12.8 cm PAK 44 gun
Armour: Maximum 250 mm, minimum 30 mm
Maximum speed: 24 mph
Combat radius: 68 miles
Ammunition stowage: 40 rounds

Nashorn Tank Destroyer Production began in 1943 and in general the Nashorn was an efficient weapon.
Crew: Four
Armament: One 8.8 cm PAK 43/1 gun
Armour: Maximum 30 mm, minimum 10 mm
Maximum speed: 25 mph
Combat radius: 125 miles
Ammunition stowage: 25 rounds

Armoured Cars

SdKfz 221 & 222 Light Armoured Cars
Crew: Two
Armament: One 7.92 mm mg, later one 2 cm KwK 30 gun as well
Armour: Maximum 15 mm, minimum 5 mm
Maximum speed: 50 mph
Combat radius: 200 miles

SdKfz 231 Armoured Car (six wheeled)
Crew: Four

Armament: One 7.92 mm mg or one 20 mm cannon
Armour: Maximum 15 mm, minimum 8 mm
Maximum speed: 38 mph
Combat radius: 250 miles

SdKfz 232, 233 & 234 Armoured Cars (eight wheeled) The initial variant of this series of eight wheeled armoured cars was originally given the 231 number of the six wheelers. The radio variant became the 232, the 233 had a short 75 mm gun, whilst the 234 was a much improved version with an air cooled engine and thicker armour.

SdKfz 232
Crew: Four
Armament: One 2 cm automatic cannon and one 7.92 mm mg
Armour: Maximum 15 mm, minimum 8 mm
Maximum speed: 53 mph
Combat radius: 170 miles

SdKfz 234
As 232, with following variations:
Armament: One short 5 cm KwK 39 gun as Puma variant
Armour: Maximum 30 mm, minimum 9 mm
Combat radius: 625 miles

ARTILLERY

Self-propelled artillery

Brummbar Assault Gun   Also known as the Sturmpanzer, the Brummbar was a heavy support weapon based on the PzKpfw IV chassis and first appeared in April 1943.
Crew: Five
Armament: One 15 cm StuH 43
Armour: Maximum 100 mm, minimum 10 mm
Maximum speed: 25 mph
Combat radius: 130 miles
Ammunition stowage: 38 rounds

Hummel Self-Propelled Gun   Intended to provide heavy artillery support to armoured formations, the Hummel came into service too late for this role and was used largely as an assault gun.
Crew: Six
Armament: One 15 cm FH 18 howitzer
Armour: Maximum 20 mm, minimum 10 mm
Maximum speed: 25 mph

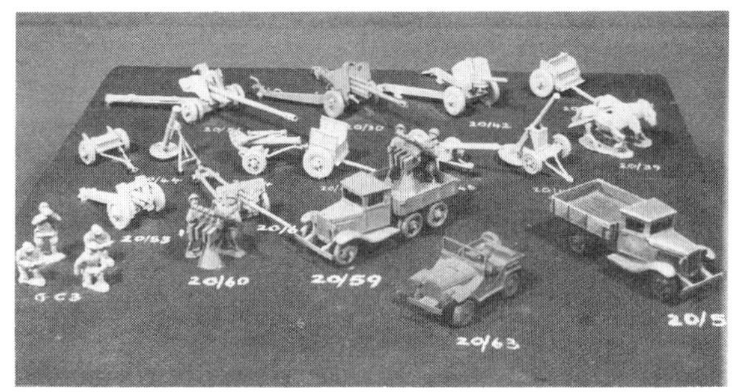

Russian equipment in 20mm from Hinchliffe Models (Photo: Steve Cox).

Combat radius: 120 miles
Ammunition stowage: 18 rounds

Marder Self-Propelled Gun In all three self-propelled guns bearing the name Marder saw service, but all were different. The Marder I was based on a French APC, the II on the PzKpfw II and III used the Czech TNHP chassis.
Crew: (I) Five (II) Three (III) Four
Armament: (I–III) 7.5 cm PAK 40 gun
Armour: Maximum (I) 12 mm (II) 30 mm (III) 15 mm, minimum (I & II) 5 mm (III) 8 mm
Maximum speed: (I) 21 mph (II) 25 mph (III) 26 mph
Combat radius: (I) 85 (II & III) 120 miles
Ammunition stowage: (I) 30 (II) 37 (III) 27 rounds

Panzerwerfer 42 Self-Propelled Rocket Launcher This weapon was the result of the Germans' wish to mobilise their successful Nebelwerfer rocket launcher.
Crew: Three
Armament: One ten barrelled 15 cm Nebelwerfer
Armour: Maximum 10 mm, minimum 6 mm
Maximum speed: 25 mph
Combat radius: 80 miles
Ammunition stowage: 20 rockets

Schweresinfanteriegeschutz Self-Propelled Gun Designed to provide a mobile platform for the highly rated 15 cm SIG33 howitzer, this self-propelled gun had several chassis variants. The 1942 version was based on the Czech TNHP chassis and is detailed here.
Crew: Four
Armament: One 15 cm SIG33 howitzer
Armour: Maximum 15 mm, minimum 8 mm
Maximum speed: 21 mph
Combat radius: 125 miles
Ammunition stowage: 18 rounds

Sturmgeschutz III Assault Gun Based on the hull of PzKpfw III, the Stug III was one of the most successful of all the German assault guns with a total of nearly 8,000 being produced in various marks.

Ausf G
Crew: Four
Armament: One 7.5 cm PAK 40 gun
Armour: Maximum 80 mm, minimum 16 mm
Maximum speed: 25 mph
Combat radius: 100 miles
Ammunition stowage: 54 rounds

Sturmgeschutze IV Assault Gun This time based on the PzKpfw IV, the Stug IV performed as well as the Stug III.
Crew: Four
Armament: One 7.5 mm PAK 40 gun
Armour: Maximum 80 mm, minimum 10 mm
Maximum speed: 24 mph
Combat radius: 130 miles
Ammunition stowage: 63 rounds

Sturmmorser 38 Self-Propelled Rocket Launcher The Sturmmorser came into being in response to the request for a very heavy, yet mobile, mortar.
Crew: Five
Armament: One 38 cm rocket launcher
Armour: Maximum 150 mm, minimum 25 mm
Maximum speed: 25 mph
Combat radius: 75 miles
Ammunition stowage: 14 rounds

Wespe Self-Propelled Gun
Crew: Five
Armament: One to 10.5 cm leFH 18 howitzer
Armour: Maximum 20 mm, minimum 10 mm

A 54mm model of the German 105mm Howitzer and crew from Hinchliffe Models (Photo: Steve Cox).

Maximum speed: 25 mph
Combat radius: 87 miles
Ammunition stowage: 32 rounds

Wirbelwind Anti-aircraft Gun Based on the PzKpfw IV, the Wirbelwind was
the only quad 20 mm vehicle to go into production.
Crew: Five
Armament: Four 2 cm Flak 36 automatic guns
Armour: Maximum 80 mm, minimum 16 mm
Maximum speed: 24 mph
Combat radius: 125 miles
Ammunition stowage: 3,200 rounds

Towed Artillery

Anti-tank artillery
5 cm PAK 38 could penetrate 86 mm at 500 yards
7.5 cm PAK 40 could penetrate 115 mm at 500 yards
8.8 cm PAK 43 could penetrate 226 mm at 500 yards

Infantry Guns
7.5 cm IG L/13 maximum range 3,840
7.5 cm IG37 maximum range 5,150
7.5 cm IG42 maximum range 4,600

Field artillery
7.5 cm leFK18 maximum range 9,425
7.5 cm FK38 maximum range 11,500
10.5 cm leFH18 maximum range 11,680
10.5 cm leFH18M maximum range 14,500
10.5 cm leFH42 maximum range 13,000

Heavy artillery
15 cm sFH18 maximum range 14,600
15 cm sFH36 maximum range 12,300
15 cm K18 maximum range 27,000
17 cm K18 maximum range 29,600
17 cm K18M maximum range 32,000
21 cm Morser 18 maximum range 16,700

Anti-aircraft artillery
5 cm Flak41 maximum range 9,000
8.8 cm Flak41 maximum range 15,000

INFANTRY WEAPONS

Rifle: Mauser Karabiner 98K 7.92 mm

Machine guns: The Germans were the first army to adopt the general purpose machine gun. The MG34 and MG42, the two main types used during the war, were considered as being "light" when mounted on a bipod and "heavy" when a tripod was used.

Anti-tank (A/t): Panzerbusche 38 7.92 mm could penetrate 30 mm at 100 yards, Panzerfaust 1943 could penetrate 203 mm up to 100 metres.

Mortar: 5 cm Leichter Granatwerfer 36 1.9 lb bomb, 550 yards. 8 cm Schwerer Granatwerfer 34 7.7 lb bomb, 2,600 yards.

Italy

ARMOURED VEHICLES

Tanks

CV 33 Tankette Limited in use by the time of the war, the Tankette was based on the Carden-Lloyd tankette of 1929 vintage.
Crew: Two
Armament: One or two 6.5 mm mgs, or one 13 mm hmg
Armour: Maximum 8 mm
Maximum speed: 26 mph
Combat radius: 78 miles
Ammunition stowage: 2,240 rounds

Fiat 300 Light Tank Based on the French Renault FT-17 light tank, the Fiat was the only tank serving in any numbers in the Italian army, although badly outdated by the time of the war.
Crew: Two
Armament: Two 6.5 mm mgs, or one 37 mm gun and one 6.5 mm mg
Armour: Maximum 16 mm, minimum 6 mm
Maximum speed: 15 mph
Combat radius: 59 miles
Ammunition stowage: 60 rounds

L6/40 Light Tank The L6/40 was developed from the tankettes of the early 1930s. Not available in significant numbers until 1942, the L6/40 saw service in North Africa.
Crew: Two
Armament: One 20 mm Breda cannon, one 8 mm mg
Armour: Maximum 30 mm, minimum 6 mm
Maximum speed: 26 mph
Combat radius: 124 miles
Ammunition stowage: 280 rounds for 20 mm, 1,056 for mg

1/200 scale vehicles from Skytrex in a wargame situation (Photo: Steve Cox).

M13/40 Medium Tank The M13/40 was the main Italian battle tank.
Crew: Four
Armament: One 47 mm gun, three 8 mm mgs
Armour: Maximum 40 mm, minimum 14 mm
Maximum speed: 20 mph
Combat radius: 125 miles
Ammunition stowage: 104 47 mm rounds, 3,048 mg

ARMOURED CARS
AB40 Armoured Car
Crew: Four
Armament: Three 8 mm mgs
Armour: Maximum 9 mm
Maximum speed: 47 mph
Combat radius: 250 miles
Ammunition stowage: 4,008 rounds

ARTILLERY
Self-Propelled artillery
Semovente 75/18 Self-Propelled Gun The 75/18 provided the main artillery
support for the Italian armoured divisons in North Africa and Sicily.
Crew: Four
Armament: One Model 1935 75/18 75 mm howitzer and one 6.5 mm
mg
Armour: Maximum 30 mm, minimum 6 mm
Maximum speed: 22 mph
Combat radius: 125 miles
Ammunition stowage: 48 rounds

Semovente 47/32 su L 6/40 Self-Propelled Gun This gun provided the out-
dated anti-tank support for the Italians in the Western Desert.
Crew: Three
Armament: One 47/32 47 mm anti-tank gun and one 6.5 mm mg

Two 25mm German Panther tanks advance on the author's wargames table.

Armour: Maximum 30 mm, minimum 6 mm
Maximum speed 26 mph
Combat radius: 125 miles
Ammunition stowage: 89 rounds

Semovente 90/53 su M41 Self-Propelled Gun Providing anti-tank support for the Italians from 1942, the 90/53 gun carried by this vehicle was almost a match for the German 88.
Crew: Four
Armament: One Model 1939 90/53 90 mm gun
Armour: Maximum 40 mm, minimum 10 mm

Maximum speed: 22 mph
Combat radius: 125 miles
Ammunition stowage: 6 rounds

Towed Artillery

Anti-tank artillery
Canone da 47/32 M35 could penetrate 43 mm at 550 yards
Canone da 47/32 Mo.39 maximum range 7,000

Field artillery
75/27 Mo. '06 maximum range 6,800
75/32 Mo. 37 maximum range 12,500
75/38 maximum range 13,000
Obice da 75/18 Mo. 35 maximum range 9,400

Heavy artillery
Canone da 149/40 Mo. 35 maximum range 22,000
Obice da 149/19 Mo. 37/41/42 maximum range 16,740
Obice da 210/22 Mo. 35 maximum range 16,000

Anti-aircraft artillery
75/46 Mo. 35 Ansoldo maximum range 9,300
90/53 Ansoldo maximum range 12,000

INFANTRY WEAPONS

Rifle: Mannlicher-Parravincino Carcano Modello 91 6.5 mm
Smg: 9 mm Beretta Modello 1938A
Lmg: 6.5 mm Breda Modello 1930
Hmg: 6.5 mm Fiat-Revelli Modello 1914
A/t: Polish Wz35 Marosczek 7.92 mm could penetrate 20 mm at 300 yards
Mortar: 45 mm Modello 35 Brixia 1 lb bomb, 550 yards
           81 mm Modello 35 7.2 lb bomb, 4,400 yards

Japan

ARMOURED VEHICLES

Tanks

Type 89 Medium Tank
Crew: Four
Armament: One 57 mm gun, two 6.5 mm mgs
Armour: Maximum 17 mm, minimum 10 mm
Maximum speed: 17 mph
Combat radius: 100 miles

Type 94 Tankette
Crew: Two
Armament: One 6.5 mm mg
Armour: Maximum 12 mm, minimum 4 mm
Maximum speed: 25 mph
Combat radius: 130 miles

Type 95 Light Tank
Crew: Three
Armament: One 37 mm gun, two 7.7 mm mgs
Armour: Maximum 12 mm, minimum 6 mm
Maximum speed: 28 mph
Combat radius: 155 miles

Type 97 Medium tank
Crew: Four
Armament: One 57 mm gun, two 7.7 mm mgs
Armour: Maximum 25 mm, minimum 8 mm
Maximum speed: 25 mph
Combat radius: 130 miles

Type 97 Tankette
Crew: Two

Armament: One 37 mm gun
Armour: Maximum 12 mm, minimum 6 mm
Maximum speed: 26 mph
Combat radius: 155 miles

Armoured Cars

Osaka Armoured Car
Crew: Three
Armament: One or two 6.5 mm mgs
Armour: Maximum 10 mm
Maximum speed: 37 mph
Combat radius: 150 miles

Sumida Armoured Car Type 2593
Crew: Six
Armament: One 6.5 mm mg
Armour: Maximum 10 mm
Maximum speed: 37 mph
Combat radius: 150 miles

ARTILLERY

Towed artillery

Anti-tank artillery
37 mm Mod94 could penetrate 24 mm at 1,000 yards
47 mm Type 1 could penetrate 50 mm at 500 yards

Field artillery
75 mm Field Gun Meiji 38 maximum range 8,250
75 mm Field Gun Model 90 maximum range 16,350
105 mm Howitzer Model 91 maximum range 11,780
105 mm Gun Type 38 maximum range 11,000
105 mm Gun-Howitzer Type 92 maximum range 20,000

Heavy artillery
15 cm Gun Model 90 maximum range 19,900
15 cm Howitzer Model 96 maximum range 11,850

INFANTRY WEAPONS

Rifle: Type 99 Arisaka 7.7 mm
Smg: Type 100 8 mm
Lmg: Type 96 6.5 mm, Type 99 7.7 mm
Hmg: Type 92 7.7 mm

A lone 25mm Tiger tank seeking its prey!

Mortar: Type 89 50 mm 1.75 lb bomb, 700 yards
Type 97 81 mm 7 lb bomb, 2,200 yards

Poland

ARMOURED VEHICLES

Tanks

TK-3 Tankette
Crew: Two
Armament: One 7.92 mm mg
Armour: Maximum 8 mm
Maximum speed: 28 mph
Combat radius: 125 miles
Ammunition stowage: 1,000 rounds

7TP Light Tank
Crew: Three
Armament: One Bofors 37 mm gun, one 7.92 mm mg
Armour: Maximum 40 mm, minimum 8 mm
Maximum speed: 20 mph
Combat radius: 100 miles
Ammunition stowage: 37 mm 80 rounds, 5,940 mg

Armoured Cars

Ursus Wz 29 Armoured Car
Crew: Five or six
Armament: One 37 mm Puteaux gun, two mgs

INFANTRY WEAPONS

The bulk of the Polish infantry weapons were of French origin.
At: Wz35 Marosczek 7.92 mm, could penetrate 20 mm at 300 yards

The Soviet Union

ARMOURED VEHICLES

Tanks

BT-7 Fast Tank The fast tank was the Russian solution to the need for a tank to operate behind enemy lines—the armoured equivalent perhaps of light cavalry—but one that was heavily outclassed by German tanks.
Crew: Three
Armament: One 45 mm M1935 gun and one 7.62 mm Degtyarev mg
Armour: Maximum 22 mm, minimum 10 mm
Maximum speed: 46 mph
Combat radius: 270 miles
Ammunition stowage: 172 rounds

IS-3 Heavy Tank Conceived as an answer to the German 88 mm gun, variants of this tank stayed in service until 1970.
Crew: Four
Armament: One 122 mm D-25 L/43 gun, one 7.62 mm mg and one a/a 12.7 mm mg
Armour: Maximum 132 mm, minimum 19 mm
Maximum speed: 23 mph
Combat radius: 94 miles
Ammunition stowage: 28 rounds

KV-1 Heavy Tank The KV series of tanks was designed to defeat fixed defensive positions and to provide infantry support.
Crew: Five
Armament: One 76.2 mm M1939 gun, later, one 85 mm M1944 gun, and three 7.62 mm mgs.
Armour: Maximum 77 mm, minimum 40 mm.
Maximum speed: 22 mph
Combat radius: 156 miles
Ammunition stowage: 114 rounds

A Hinchliffe model of a German medium field gun in 1/72 scale.

The KV-II was identical, apart from the fact that it mounted a D-10 152 mm howitzer in a huge box-like turret.

T-26 Light Tank
Crew: Three
Armament: A number of combinations; two 7.62 mm mgs, or one 37 mm gun and a 7.62 mm mg, or one 45 mm gun and a 7.62 mm mg, or a flame-thrower and a 7.62 mm mg
Armour: Maximum 25 mm, minimum 6 mm
Maximum speed: 17 mph
Combat radius: 140 miles
Ammunition stowage: 165 rounds

T-28 Medium Tank
Crew: Six
Armament: One 76.2 mm gun, three 7.62 mm mgs
Armour: Maximum 80 mm, minimum 20 mm
Maximum speed: 23 mph
Combat radius: 140 miles
Ammunition stowage: 70 rounds

T-34 Medium Tank
The T-34 is widely believed to be the best tank of the war, if not the 20th century. Certainly, it was the Russians' main battle tank and a major factor in the defeat of the Germans.
Crew: Five
Armament: One 76.2 mm Model 1939 L-11 gun, later one 85 mm D-5T gun, and two 7.62 mm mgs
Armour: Maximum 60 mm, minimum 18 mm
Maximum speed: 31 mph
Combat radius: 186 miles
Ammunition stowage: 80 rounds

T-60 Light Tank
Crew: Two
Armament: One 20 mm and one 7.62 mm mg
Armour: Maximum 20 mm, minimum 7 mm
Maximum speed: 28 mph
Combat radius: 382 miles
Ammunition stowage: 780 rounds

T-70 Light Tank
Crew: Two
Armament: One 45 mm gun, one 7.62 mm mg
Armour: Maximum 60 mm, minimum 10 mm
Maximum speed: 37 mph

Combat radius: 310 miles
Ammunition stowage: 70 rounds

Armoured Cars

BA-10
Crew: Four
Armament: One 45 mm gun, two 7.62 mm mgs
Armour: Maximum 15 mm, minimum 6 mm
Maximum speed: 35 mph
Combat radius: 190 miles
Ammunition stowage: Unknown

BA-64 Armoured Car
Crew: Two
Armament: One 7.62 mg
Armour: Maximum 10 mm, minimum 6 mm
Maximum speed: 50 mph
Combat radius: 375 miles
Ammunition stowage: Unknown

ARTILLERY

Self-Propelled artillery

ISU-22 Self-Propelled Gun Designed to support the IS series of heavy tanks, the ISU-22 was built initially on a KV-1 chassis and subsequently, that of an IS. The gun is still in service today.
Crew: Five
Armament: One Model 1944 D-25S L/43 122 mm gun, one a/a 12.7 mm mg
Armour: Maximum 110 mm, minimum 20 mm
Maximum speed: 22 mph
Combat radius: 150 miles
Ammunition stowage: 30 rounds

ISU-152 Self-Propelled Gun The ISU-152 was closely akin to the ISU-22, apart from the gun.
Armament: One Model 1944 ML-20S 152 mm gun, one 12.7 mm a/a mg

SU-76 Light Self-Propelled Gun Based on the T-70 chassis, this SP came into service in 1942 to provide firepower for armoured formations.
Crew: Four
Armament: One 76.2 mm Model 1942 (215-3) gun
Armour: Maximum 35 mm, minimum 10 mm

An Airfix model in 1/72 scale of a German Stugg III self propelled gun with a short barrelled 7.5cm gun.

Maximum speed: 28 mph
Combat radius: 166 miles
Ammunition stowage: 60 rounds

SU-85 Medium Self-Propelled Gun The emergence of the German Panther and Tiger tanks forced the Russians to seek a counter-measure. The SU-85, based on a T-34 chassis, provided the solution.
Crew: Four
Armament: One Model 1943 D5-85 85 mm gun
Armour: Maximum 54 mm, minimum 20 mm
Maximum speed: 30 mph
Combat radius: 200 miles
Ammunition stowage: 48 rounds

SU-100 Medium Self-Propelled Gun The T-34 chassis, married to an ex-naval 100 mm gun produced the SU-100, a most effective tank destroyer.
Crew: Four
Armament: One Model 1944 (D-10S) 100 mm gun
Armour: Maximum 54 mm, minimum 20 mm
Maximum speed: 30 mph
Combat radius: 200 miles
Ammunition stowage: Unknown

Towed Artillery

Anti-tank artillery
45 mm Model 1932 could penetrate 38 mm at 1,000 yards
57 mm Model 1941 could penetrate 140 mm at 500 yards
100 mm Model 1944 could penetrate 200 mm at 450 yards

Field artillery
76 mm Divisional Gun M33 range 13,600
76 mm Gun ZIS-3 maximum range 13,000
76.2 mm Model 1939 maximum range 14,500

A white metal model kit of a Dingo scout car in 1/72 scale.

A resin model of a Canadian Ram Badger flame throwing tank from Cromwell Models.

85 mm Model 1943 maximum range 18,000
122 mm Howitzer M38 maximum range, 11,795

Heavy artillery
107 mm Model 1910/30r maximum range 18,000
107 mm Model 1940 M 60 maximum range 18,000
122 mm Corps Gun M31/37 (A-19) maximum range 20,800
152 mm Howitzer M-10 maximum range 12,400
152 mm Gun Howitzer ML-20 maximum range 17,280

Anti-aircraft artillery
76.2 mm M31 maximum range 9,500
85 mm M39 maximum range 8,280

INFANTRY WEAPONS

Rifle: Model 1891/30g Mosin Nagant 7.62 mm
Smg: 7.62 mm PPSh-1941
Lmg: 7.62 mm Degtyarev DP1928
Hmg: 7.62 mm Model PM1910 Goryunov SG43
A/t: Degtyarev 14.5 mm PTRD 1941 could penetrate 25 mm at 500 yards
Mortar: 50 mm PM41, 3,000 yards

The United Kingdom
ARMOURED VEHICLES

Tanks

Cruiser Tanks Marks 1-4 The concept of the cruiser tank sweeping around the enemy's flanks and hitting deep behind his lines—much in the manner of the naval namesake—appealed to the British army. Many of the initial marks were produced and saw active service, it is only fitting that they are noted here, albeit in a summarised format.
Crew: Six (Mark 1) Five (Mark 2) Four (Marks 3 & 4)
Armament: (1) 2pdr, three mgs. (2) 2pdr, two mgs. (3 & 4) 2pdr. one mg.

Armour: Maximum (1, 2 & 4) 30 mm (3) 14 mm
         minimum (1 & 3) 6 mm (2) 10 mm (4) 20 mm
Maximum speed: (1) 25 (2) 15 (3) 30 (4) 28 mph
Combat radius: (1, 2 & 4) 95 (3) 108 miles
Ammunition stowage: (1, 2 & 3) 2pdr 100 rounds, (1) 3,000 mg (2) 4.050 mg (3) 3,750 mg.
Note that the Mark 1 is also referred to as the A9, the Mark 2 as the A10, the Mark 3 as the A13 and the Mark 4 as the A13 second version.

Centaur Cruiser Tank
Crew: Five
Armament: One 6pdr gun, or one 75 mm gun, or one 95 mm howitzer and two 7.92 mm Besa mgs
Armour: Maximum 76 mm, minimum 20 mm
Maximum speed: 27 mph
Combat radius: 185 miles
Ammunition stowage: 51 rounds, 4,950 mg

Challenger Cruiser Tank
Crew: Five
Armament: One 17pdr gun, one 7.92 mm Besa mg
Armour: Maximum 100 mm, minimum 20 mm
Maximum speed: 31 mph
Combat radius: 135 miles
Ammunition stowage: 42 rounds

Churchill Infantry Tank Designed as an infantry support vehicle, the Churchill served throughout the war in this role and its chassis provided the basis for a number of specialised conversions.
Crew: Five
Armament: One 2 pdr, or one 6 pdr, or one 75 mm gun, or one 95 mm howitzer (early models featured a hull mounted 3" howitzer) and two 7.92 mm Besa mgs
Armour: Maximum 101 mm, minimum 50 mm
Combat radius: 88 miles
Ammunition stowage: 84 rounds 6 pdr, 6,975 mg

Comet Cruiser Tank The Comet tank was in fact the Cromwell tank hull with a new turret to accommodate a larger gun.
Crew: Five
Armament: One 77 mm gun, two 7.92 mm Besa mgs
Armour: Maximum 101 mm, minimum 14 mm
Maximum speed: 31 mph
Combat radius: 125 miles
Ammunition stowage: 61 rounds 77 mm, 5,175 mg

Cromwell Heavy Cruiser Tank The Cromwell was the last and arguably the best of the Cruiser series of tanks.
Crew: Five
Armament: One 6 pdr, or 75 mm gun, or one 75 mm howitzer, two 7.92 mm Besa mgs
Armour: Maximum 102 mm, minimum 8 mm
Combat radius: 170 miles
Ammunition stowage: 64 rounds 75 mm, 4,950 mg

Crusader Cruiser Tank The Crusader provided the main part of the British armoured formations until replaced by the M3 and M4 tanks (see USA section).
Crew: Five
Armament: One 2 pdr, later one 6 pdr gun, two or three 7.92 mm Besa mgs
Armour: Maximum 50 mm, minimum 7 mm
Maximum speed: 28 mph
Combat radius: 200 miles
Ammunition stowage: 65 rounds 6 pdr, 5,000 mg

Firefly Tank The gun on the M4 Sherman was not sufficiently powerful to knock out the German Panther and Tiger tanks. Accordingly the British modified the M4 to accept their new 17 pdr anti-tank gun. Since in all other details the tank was a Sherman, this will be largely covered in the US section.
Armament: One 17 pdr gun Mk1.

Matilda Infantry Tanks 1-3 The thick armour of the Matildas served them well, causing the Germans to up-gun rapidly and remaining proof against any Japanese anti-tank gun throughout the war. The Matildas were used by the Australians and were particularly important in the Western Desert until replaced by the M3 and M4 tanks.
Crew: (Matilda 1) Two, (Matilda 2 & 3) Four
Armament: (1) One .303, later .50, Vickers mg (2 & 3) One 2 pdr gun, one 7.92 mm Besa mg, or one 3" howitzer and one 7.92 mm mg
Armour: Maximum (1) 60 mm (2 & 3) 78 mm, minimum (1) 10 mm (2 & 3) 14 mm
Maximum speed: (1) 8 (2 & 3) 15 mph
Combat radius: (1) 78 (2) 155 (3) 160 miles
Ammunition stowage: (1) 4,000 rounds (2 & 3) 92 rounds 6 pdr, 2,925 mg

Valentine Infantry Tank First appearing in May 1940, the Valentine eventually had eleven different marks and was used as the basis for a number of specialised vehicles. The Valentine was also used by Australian and Canadian forces.

Mark III

Crew: Three or four
Armament: 2 pdr, 6 pdr or 75 mm gun, one 7.62 or 7.92 mg
Armour: Maximum 65 mm, minimum 8 mm
Maximum speed: 15 mph
Combat radius: 90 miles
Ammunition stowage: 2 pdr 79 rounds, 6 pdr 53 rounds, 75 mm 50 rounds

Vickers Light Tank   The Vickers Light tank formed the bulk of the British armour in France in 1940, the Mark VIB being the most numerous.

Mark VIB

Crew: Three
Armament: One .5" and one .303" mg
Armour: Maximum 14 mm, minimum 4 mm
Maximum speed: 35 mph
Combat radius: 130 miles
Ammunition stowage: Unknown

Tank Destroyers

Archer Tank Destroyer   When the 17 pdr gun came into service in 1942, the hull and chassis of the Valentine was used to provide it with mobility.
Crew: Four
Armament: One 17 pdr gun Mk1
Armour: Maximum 60 mm, minimum 8 mm
Maximum speed: 20 mph
Combat radius: 100 miles
Ammunition stowage: 39 rounds

Deacon Tank Destroyer   Essentially a 6 pdr gun mounted on the chassis of a Matador lorry, the Deacon served throughout the latter part of the war in the Western Desert.

The Airfix kit of the British Crusader Mk III tank.

Crew: Four
Armament: One 6 pdr gun Mk 1
Armour: 10 mm
Maximum speed: 25 mph
Combat radius: 155 miles
Ammunition stowage: 24 rounds

Armoured Cars

AEC Armoured Car
Crew: Three or four
Armament: One 2 pdr, 6 pdr or 75 mm gun
Armour: Maximum 57 mm, minimum 7 mm
Maximum speed: 40 mph
Combat radius: 250 miles
Ammunition stowage: Unknown

Daimler Armoured Car
The most popular British armoured car of the war, the Daimler saw much service in Europe and North Africa after its entry on to the scene in 1941, as well as after the war.
Crew: Three
Armament: One 2 pdr gun
Armour: 16 mm
Maximum speed: 50 mph
Combat radius: 205 miles
Ammunition stowage: Unknown

Humber Armoured Car
Crew: Three
Armament: One 15 mm Besa hmg, (later, 37 mm gun) and one 7.92 mm mg
Armour: 15 mm
Maximum speed: 45 mph
Combat radius: 250 miles
Ammunition stowage: Unknown

The American "Buffalo" amphibious vehicle with the ubiquitous Jeep.

Reconnaissance Vehicles

Daimler Dingo Light Armoured Scout Car The Dingo was widely used during the war and is still in service today.
Crew: Two
Armament: One .303in Bren mg
Armour: Maximum 30mm, minimum 10mm
Maximum speed: 55mph
Combat radius: 200 miles
Ammunition stowage: Unknown

The Bren Carrier This most useful vehicle was a great deal of service and was used as a basis for a great many adaptions.
Crew: Two
Armament: .303in Bren mg, or .55in Boys anti-tank rifle
Maximum speed: 30mph

The subsequent Universal Carrier was based on the Bren Carrier and offered a basis for the conversions which had been unsuccessful with the Bren. A good many Bren Carriers were enhanced to Universal standards and in common parlance all the carriers were referred to as "Bren".

ARTILLERY

Self-Propelled artillery

The Bishop Based on the chassis of a Valentine, the Bishop provided mobility for the 25pdr gun.
Crew: Four
Armament: One 25pdr gun Mk2
Armour: Maximum 60mm, minimum 8mm
Maximum speed: 15mph
Combat radius: 90 miles
Ammunition stowage: 32 rounds

Towed Artillery

Anti-tank artillery
2pdr Mk 9 could penetrate 53mm at 500 yards
6pdr Mk2 could penetrate 70mm at 1,000 yards
17pdr Mk1 could penetrate 130mm at 1,000 yards

Field artillery
3.7" Pack howitzer maximum range 6,000
25pdr Mk2 maximum range 12,250

4.5" Howitzer Mk1 maximum range 6,675
4.5" Gun Mk2 maximum range 18,745
5.5" Gun Mk3 maximum range 17,145
6" Gun Mk19 maximum range 17,145

Heavy artillery
7.2" Howitzer Mk6 maximum range 17,925

Anti-aircraft artillery
3" 20 cwt Mk1 maximum range 11,330
3.7" Mk6 maximum range 18,075

INFANTRY WEAPONS

Rifle: .303" Short Magazine Lee Enfield Mark 3
Smg: 9 mm Sten gun
Lmg: .303" Bren, .303" Lewis gun
Hmg: .303" Vickers
A/t: Boys A/t Rifle, could penetrate 25 mm at 500 yards.
    PIAT, could penetrate 75 mm at 500 yards
Mortar: 2" 2.25 lb bomb, 500 yards
        3" 10 lb bomb, 2,000 yards

The United States

ARMOURED VEHICLES

Tanks

M3 Medium Tank Lee/Grant Referred to as the General Grant in British service (due to a turret modification to take a radio) and as the General Lee in American service, the M3 served throughout the desert war and was used by the Australians.
Crew: Six
Armament: One hull sponson mounted Browning 75 mm gun M2 and one turret mounted 37 mm gun M5, three .30 Browning mgs
Armour: Maximum 57 mm, minimum 12 mm
Maximum speed: 26 mph
Combat radius: 120 miles
Ammunition stowage: 46 rounds 75 mm, 178 rounds 37 mm, 9,200 mg

M3/M5 Light Tank Called the General Stuart in British service, the M3 had several improvements made to it before becoming the M3A3. A new engine was fitted and the tank re-designated M5, but remained the same as the M3A3 in all other aspects.

The PzKpfw III tank, made from the Airfix 1/72 kit.

A model of the Matilda MkII infantry tank.

M3A3

Crew: Four
Armament: One 37 mm gun M5, then M6 and two .30 Browning mgs
Armour: Maximum 38 mm, minimum 12 mm
Maximum speed: 36 mph
Combat radius: 70 miles
Ammunition stowage: 116 rounds 37 mm, 8,270 mg

M4 Medium Tank Sherman The Sherman became for many years the main battle tank of the Allied armies. Many updating versions were produced and the tank remains in service today, in all nearly 50,000 were made. For our purposes here, the M4A3 has been taken as a representative variant.

M4A3

Crew: Five
Armament: One 75 mm gun M3, two .30 mgs and one .50 mg
Armour: Maximum 108 mm, minimum 12 mm
Maximum speed: 26 mph
Combat radius: 100 miles
Ammunition stowage: 71 rounds 76 mm, 6,250 .30", 600 .5" mgs

M24 Light Tank Chaffee Designed to replace the ageing M3/M5 light tank series, the M24 did not go into production until April 1944.
Crew: Five
Armament: One 75 mm gun M6 and two .30 mgs
Armour: Maximum 38 mm, minimum 12 mm
Maximum speed: 30 mph
Combat radius: 100 miles
Ammunition stowage: 48 rounds 75 mm, 4,125 .30", 420 .5" mgs

M26 Heavy Tank Pershing Another late arrival, the Pershing entered service in March 1945 to counter the German heavy tanks.
Crew: Five
Armament: One 90 mm gun M3, two .30 and one .50 Browning mgs

ESCI plastic model of the German PzKpfw 38T, an earlier war tank.

A British Morris artillery prime mover, modelled from an Airfix kit.

Armour: Maximum 102 mm, minimum 51 mm
Maximum speed: 30 mph
Combat radius: 110 miles
Ammunition stowage: 70 rounds 90 mm, 5,000 .3", 550 .5" mgs

Tank Destroyers

M10 Gun Motor Carriage Known as the Achilles in British service, the M10 appeared in every war theatre.
Crew: Five
Armament: One 3" gun M7
Armour: Maximum 57 mm, minimum 10 mm
Maximum speed: 30 mph
Combat radius: 200 miles
Ammunition stowage: 54 rounds

M18 Gun Motor Carriage (Hellcat)
Crew: Five
Armament: One 76 mm gun M1A1
Armour: Maximum 25 mm, minimum 12 mm
Maximum speed: 50 mph
Combat radius: 150 miles
Ammunition stowage: 45 rounds

Armoured Cars

M8 Greyhound Armoured Car The most widely used American armoured car and many remain in use still.
Crew: Four
Armament: One 37 mm gun M6
Armour: Maximum 20 mm, minimum 6 mm
Maximum speed: 55 mph
Combat radius: 350 miles
Ammunition stowage: 80 rounds

T17E1 Staghound Armoured Car
Crew: Five
Armament: One 37 mm M6 gun
Armour: Maximum 45 mm, minimum 9 mm
Maximum speed: 56 mph
Combat radius: 450 miles
Ammunition stowage: 103 rounds

Reconnaissance Vehicles

M3A1 White Scout Car
Crew: Two
Armament: One .50 and one .30 mgs
Armour: 7 mm
Maximum speed: 50 mph
Combat radius: 250 miles
Ammunition stowage: Unknown
Note: The M3A1 could carry up to six passengers, in addition to the two crew members.

ARTILLERY

Self-Propelled artillery

M3 Motor Gun Carriage Essentially, this equipment was a 75 mm gun on a GMC half-track.
Crew: Five
Armament: One 75 mm M1897A4 gun
Armour: Maximum 12 mm, minimum 6 mm
Maximum speed: 45 mph
Combat radius: 200 miles
Ammunition stowage: 59 rounds

M7 Howitzer Motor Carriage Called the Priest by the British, the M7 went into service in April 1942.
Crew: Seven
Armament: 105 mm howitzer M2A1
Armour: Maximum 108 mm, minimum 12 mm
Maximum speed: 24 mph
Combat radius: 120 miles
Ammunition stowage: 69 rounds

M8 Howitzer Motor Carriage Based on the M5 light tank, the M8 provided close support for medium tank formations.
Crew: Four
Armament: One 75 mm howitzer M2

Armour: Maximum 28 mm, minimum 10 mm
Maximum speed: 35 mph
Combat radius: 130 miles
Ammunition stowage: 46 rounds

M12 Gun Motor Carriage Mounting a 155 mm gun, the M12 proved a very
effective means of providing medium artillery support to armoured
units.
Crew: Six
Armament: One 155 mm gun M1917 or 18
Armour: Maximum 50 mm, minimum 10 mm
Maximum speed: 24 mph
Combat radius: 140 miles
Ammunition stowage: 10 rounds

Towed Artillery

Anti-tank
37 mm Gun M3A1 could penetrate 25 mm at 1,000 yards
57 mm Gun M1 could penetrate 70 mm at 1,000 yards
3" M5 could penetrate 96 mm at 1,000 yards

Field artillery
75 mm M1917 maximum range 8,000
75 mm M1A1 Pack howitzer maximum range 9,750
105 mm Howitzer M2A1 maximum range 11,200

Heavy artillery
4.5" Gun M1* maximum range 18,750
155 mm Gun M1 maximum range 35,000
155 mm Gun M1918M1 maximum range 20,100
8" Howitzer M1 maximum range 18,500
8" Gun M1 maximum range 32,330

Anti-aircraft artillery
37 mm M1 maximum range 5,670
90 mm M1 maximum range 9,750

INFANTRY WEAPONS

Rifle: M1903 Springfield .30, M1 Garand .30
Smg: .45" M1928 A Thompson
Lmg: .30-06 Browning M1919 A6
Hmg: .30 Browning M1917 A1
A/t: 2.36" Rocket Launcher M1, 3.41 lb bomb, 500 yards
Mortar: 60 mm M2 2.9 lb bomb, 2,000 yards
         81 mm M1 10.6 lb bomb, 2,500 yards

3   *Rules and Scenarios*

Having studied the weaponry of the war, we now need to reflect this information in the rules by which we will be conducting our table top battles. A couple of basic guide lines are essential when formulating rules—those of distance and time.

The distance covered by a vehicle in motion and the range of a particular weapon are usually expressed in some form of linear measurement, whether it is metres, miles or yards. We need to condense these actual distances into a format which can be utilised in wargames. Clearly, a true one-to-one ratio or scale cannot be used on a wargames table which measures only say eight feet by five—to achieve a range of 800 yards or 13,000 yards would be impossible. What happens, then, is that such distances are scaled down to a manageable size using a convenient scale such as one yard being represented by one millimetre on the table top. Thus, if a particular weapon had a range of say 900 yards, its miniature counterpart would have a range of 900 millimetres. This is the system which has been used in the following rules, but equally the inch could be used as the basic unit of measurement to represent the scaled down yard.

The second consideration is that of time—just what portion of time is represented by one move or turn on the wargames table?

The Bofors 40mm anti-aircraft gun.

This British truck is typical of the numerous general purpose soft-skin vehicles in constant use during the War.

Once again, a convenient segment of time, frequently the minute, is taken and this is the unit we will be using in these rules. Thus, whatever an actual soldier was capable of doing in one minute, running 100 yards for example, then his miniature counterpart should also be able to achieve this in one move on the table top.

The stated capabilities of the various tanks, guns etc. should be treated with caution. The quoted performance figures are often those produced under factory or test conditions, making no allowance for the vagaries of actual combat conditions. Two prime examples of this are the speed of a vehicle and its capacity for ammunition stowage. The figures for maximum speeds are usually achieved on a road where the vehicle in question is able to run for a sustained period on a good, even surface. This is a far cry from the actual terrain that the vehicle will have to traverse under combat conditions and we shall not be too far out if, to obtain a combat speed, we halve the quoted maximum figure. The manufacturer's stated ammunition stowage capacity of a tank or self-propelled gun was frequently increased by its crew before the vehicle went into action. Known in the British army as "bombing up" the loading of ammunition on board frequently flaunted all safety rules, with shells being crammed into every corner in an attempt to carry as many rounds as possible. The floor of a T-34 tank for example, was composed of ammunition boxes each containing one or two rounds. While the gunner and the tank commander sat on seats coming down from the turret, the unfortunate loader had to manhandle the large shell while also trying to keep his balance on the somewhat uneven floor.

The rules which follow have been simplified to offer a relatively fast, easy-to-follow game. Should this not be to the wargamer's liking, a number of suggestions for increasing the complexity of the wargame are included at the end of the main rules. Unless otherwise stated, the 'dice' referred to are the usual six-sided type, numbered one to six.

Cromwell Model's Renault AMC 35 ACG1 light tank.

A Cromwell Models 1/72 scale M4A 3E2 'Jumbo' Sherman assault tank armed with a 75 mm gun.

Movement

In considering the distance each type of piece can cover in one wargames move, the wargamer can either generalise, as has been done here, or use the known speed of a particular vehicle. There is more than one way of doing this. Either each given speed can be scaled down on the basis of say 1 mph means 1 mm covered (thus a vehicle with a speed of 26 mph is given a table top move of 26 mm), or the given speeds can be used as a basis for comparison, i.e. an armoured car which is capable of 40 mph should be seen to move at twice the speed of a 20 mph tank. Thus, if the tank is given a 50 mm move in the wargame, the armoured car should have one of 100 mm.

Infantry 75 mm
Horsedrawn 150 mm
Lorries 400 mm
Half-tracked 450 mm
Scout cars 500 mm
Armoured cars 450 mm
Self-propelled guns 150 mm
Light tanks 300 mm
Medium tanks 150 mm
Heavy tanks 100 mm

Firing

The maximum range of each weapon is as follows:
Pistol 75 mm
Rifle 300 mm
Smg 100 mm
Lmg 500 mm
Hmg 600 mm
Light mortar minimum 75 mm, maximum 450 mm
Heavy mortar minimum 200 mm, maximum 600 mm
Light anti-tank gun/rifle 600 mm, field gun 1000 mm
Medium anti-tank gun 800 mm, field gun 1250 mm
Heavy anti-tank gun 1000 mm, field gun 1750 mm
The method of firing is as follows:

(A) SMALL ARMS

It is assumed that infantrymen will be engaging only other infantry when firing small arms. While machine gun fire, particularly that from the heavier calibre pieces, would be considered sufficient to knock out an unarmoured vehicle, in these particular rules, that task is left to the artillery.

Pistol Fire

Firing once per move, which does not affect the distance the firer can move, only a six thrown on one dice will kill at any range up to the maximum of 75mm.

Rifle Fire

May fire up to two times per move. Fire once and no movement penalty, fire twice and move is reduced to 150mm.

Range	0 to 100mm	101 to 200mm	201 to 300mm
Score needed on one dice to kill one man	4,5 or 6	5 or 6	6 only

Sub-machine Gun Fire

May fire twice per move, with same restrictions as for rifle.

Range	0 to 50mm	51 to 100mm
Score needed on one dice to kill two men	5 or 6	6 only

Light Machine Gun

May fire twice per move, but no movement is permissible if weapon fires at all.

Range	0 to 100mm	101 to 300mm	301 to 500mm
Score needed on one dice to kill two men	4, 5 or 6	5 or 6	6 only

Heavy/Medium Machine Gun

May fire twice per move, but no movement is permissible if weapon fires at all.

Range	0 to 200mm	201 to 400mm	401 to 600mm
Score needed on one dice to kill three men	4,5 or 6	5 or 6	6 only

Infantrymen moving and carrying a machine gun do not suffer any penalty in their movement. It takes a complete move to set up a light, medium or heavy machine gun which should have two crewmen. In the setting-up move there must be no other movement and no firing is permitted. Note that the "no movement if firing" rule does not apply if the machine gun is mounted in a vehicle, e.g. tank or self-propelled gun.

(B) MORTAR FIRE

Light mortars should have a crew of two figures, heavy mortars should be manned by three figures. It takes one move to assemble a light mortar, two moves for a heavy mortar. The two crewmen can carry a light mortar with a 50mm reduction applied to their move distance. The heavy mortar should be transported by a suitable vehicle—a Universal Carrier for example—whose movement rate will not be affected. In extreme circumstances, the heavy mortar can be transported by its crew at 15mm per move. Note that mortars have a minimum range below which they cannot hit targets, in addition to the usual maximum range and fire twice per move. The mortar was not particularly noted for its accuracy and, to reflect this on the table top, mortar fire is conducted in two stages.

Firstly, to establish that the correct range has been found, one ordinary dice is thrown for every 75 mm of range. The score on this dice must be equal to, or greater than, the number of 75 mm 'units' of the range, with the exception of the far end of the heavy mortar range band. This can be tabulated as follows:-

| Range to target | | Dice score required |
Light Mortar	Heavy Mortar	for hit
0 to 75 mm	0 to 200 mm	Firing not allowed
76 to 150 mm	201 to 275 mm	2 or better
151 to 225 mm	276 to 350 mm	3 or better
226 to 300 mm	351 to 425 mm	4 or better
301 to 375 mm	426 to 450 mm	5 or better
376 to 450 mm	451 to 600 mm	6 or better

Thus if the range from a light mortar to the target is 285 mm, a score of four or better would be required on the ranging dice in order for that target to be reached. A heavy mortar firing at 430 mm would need a score of 5 or better. Those shots which fall short are ignored, but if the wargamer wishes, their effect—for good or ill!—can still be calculated using the following method.

The problems do not stop once the range has been established, for we now have to consider the variance in flight of the mortar bomb. Call it windage, lateral correction or what you will, it does not follow that just because the range has been found that the bomb will hit the intended target. The basic variations to a hit are over, short, to left and to right. Granted, there are many more possible degrees of variation, but these four will suffice for our needs here. Once again, a single dice is rolled to reflect this:-

Dice score	Effect on mortar bomb
1	Falls 50 mm to left of target
2	Falls 50 mm to right of target
3	Falls 50 mm short of target
4	Falls 50 mm over target
5,6	Hits target

The quoted distance of 50 mm is fairly arbitrary, but seems a reasonable figure. The wargamer can either replace this with a differing figure if required, or create a differentiation between light and heavy mortar bombs. The effect of the misdirected bombs should still be calculated rather than ignored, in spite of it missing the intended target.

Once the mortar bomb does land it will have a varying effect, dependent on the target in question. The nature of the mortar bomb is to produce a basically circular blast—the heavier the calibre of the mortar, the greater the extent of this blast—and this is represented in the wargame as follows:-

All infantrymen within a 25 mm radius (light mortar) or 40 mm radius (heavy mortar) of the point of impact are killed. Wargamers may wish to construct paper, or even better, acetate bomb burst rings of the quoted radius in order to assist with the business of deciding just who is laid low.

Unarmoured vehicles hit by a mortar bomb are knocked out.

Anti-tank guns, field guns or mortars hit have their crews killed and the gun rendered inoperable.

Self-propelled guns were mostly open-topped and, if hit by a mortar bomb, half the crew figures will be killed which will have an adverse effect on the performance of that gun (see below).

Tanks are considered as being impervious to mortar fire.

(C) FIELD GUNS

Model field guns are crewed by two figures if light, four if medium and six if heavy. For the purposes of the wargame, field guns cannot be man-handled and move at the speed of their prime mover, be it lorry or horse team or whatever. It takes a complete move to unlimber and deploy a light or medium piece and two moves if the field gun is heavy. The guns, which fire twice per move, are assumed to be firing only high explosive shell and essentially, their fire is calculated in much the same manner as that of the mortar. On this occasion however, the range is split into six sections of approximately equal size which vary in length according to the calibre of the gun in question. To facilitate easier reference, all guns have been graded Light if they are of a calibre of up to 40 mm, Medium if they are between 41 and 77 mm and Heavy if over 78 mm:-

Range to target (in mm)			Dice score required for hit
Light Field Gun	Medium Field Gun	Heavy Field Gun	
0 to 150	0 to 200	0 to 300	automatic hit
151 to 300	201 to 400	301 to 600	2
301 to 450	400 to 600	601 to 900	3
451 to 600	601 to 800	901 to 1200	4
601 to 750	801 to 1000	1201 to 1500	5
751 to 1000	1001 to 1250	1501 to 1750	6

Whilst wargamers may wish to apply the same 'overshoot/undershoot' techniques to artillery fire, one can assume that once the range has been established using the above table, then the shell will achieve a hit. The effect on the target will vary, depending on the nature of the target and the calibre of the field gun which is firing, but

A model of the French Renault D2 infantry tank, from Cromwell Models.

The German 'run about', the Kubelwagen, from ESCI.

again we will use the 'shell burst' concept, as we did when dealing with the mortar.

Infantry

The shells of light field guns are considered to have a 40 mm effect radius, a medium 50 mm and a heavy 60 mm. Once again, the wargamer may wish to knock up some shell burst circles to these dimensions to help in casualty calculations. In any event, all infantry caught in the burst circle will be killed.

Unarmoured vehicles, if caught within one of these circles, will be knocked out by shell fire.

Anti-tank guns, field guns and mortars will also be knocked out by shell fire from medium and heavy guns. Light calibre pieces will need to roll an additional dice to establish whether or not the shell hit a vital part. A 4, 5 or 6 and it has, knocking out the target, 1, 2 or 3 and the shot has no effect.

Tanks and self-propelled guns cannot be knocked out by shell fire.

Casualties on gun crews

Should a gun or mortar crew suffer casualties, then the performance of that piece will be adversely effected. Clearly, if all the crew are killed, then the gun is out of action and cannot fire. Mortar crews may be replaced by infantrymen—one clear move must elapse after their arrival, before firing—but gun crews cannot. If a portion of the crew is killed, then the firing rate of that gun will slow down accordingly. We can say that if 25% of the crew fall, then the gun fires only once per move, 50% and it fires only every other move, 75% and it is reduced to firing every third move. The only exception to this, in order to avoid mind-blowing mental arithmetic, is the heavy mortar with its crew of three figures. Here we can use thirds—one crewman down and the mortar fires only once every move, two men down and it fires only every other move. Since unlike field gun crews, those of the mortars can be replaced, some minor book-keeping may become necessary in order to keep track of the crew status.

Benefits of cover

The casualty rates suggested above assume that the target is out in the open, but clearly the use of cover should limit the casualties sustained by one's miniature armies. Any infantry hit in cover may be saved by the throw of a 5 or 6 on one dice, with one dice being rolled for every two figures caught in the burst circle. Vehicles are less likely to be in cover, but should the need arise then it may be stipulated that a roll of 6 on one dice will mean that the vehicle in question has not actually been knocked out, but rendered unusable. The number of moves for which this condition lasts can be decided by the roll of one more dice.

(D) ANTI-TANK GUNS

The following rules apply equally to towed, self-propelled and tank mounted guns. Generally speaking, the range of an anti-tank weapon firing armour piercing solid shot or similar rounds is less than that of a similar calibre piece firing high explosive. This is mainly due to the fact that the anti-tank round relies very much on high velocity to produce the impact or 'punch' needed to penetrate the target's protective armour. The longer the range from the gun to the target, then the more the velocity of the round is lost, until finally it has no momentum at all.

The field gun on the other hand can have the benefit of timed or impact fuses, air bursts and so forth and thus is not so totally dependent on impact for its effect. As a result, the field gun is able to operate at longer ranges. Agreed, this is a simplification of the facts, but it does serve to illustrate the point and underline the very different uses and purposes of field and anti-tank artillery. Following on from this, the maximum ranges of anti-tank guns (again, tank-mounted, self-propelled or towed) are assumed to be those laid out in the following table.

As before, the guns have been divided into three types and the ranges which are expressed in millimetres, have been divided into six segments, along with the requisite score required on one 'ranging dice' to register that the range to the target has been correctly assessed.

Light Gun	Medium Gun	Heavy Gun	Dice score
0–100	0–150	0–200	Automatic hit
101–200	151–300	201–400	2
201–300	301–450	401–600	3
301–400	451–600	601–800	4
401–500	601–650	801–900	5
501–600	651–800	901–1000	6

Having considered how the range is established, we now need to examine the effect of anti-tank fire. The basic question is whether or not the fired round will penetrate the armour of the target. Back in the section on weaponry, as much information as possible was provided on penetration and we can make use of that here. The Armour Penetration Diagram given below should illustrate the general concept of the anti-tank firing mechanism.

The basic idea is that the calibre of the gun which is firing is found on the vertical scale to the left of the diagram and then the armour thickness of the intended target is similarly identified on the horizontal scale. The point at which lines drawn at right angles from each of these two origins meet is regarded as being the point of impact as the fired round hits the target. The main consideration now is whether or not the round did actually penetrate the target's armour—if the point of impact when plotted is ABOVE the plot line, then it did, if however it is BELOW that line, then it didn't. Perhaps a couple of examples will assist with the reader's understanding of the diagram's usage.

Assume that a 40 mm gun, be it tank-mounted or a deployed anti-tank gun, is firing at a fairly light tank possessing 20 mm armour. Firstly the 40 mm calibre is found on the left hand scale and a real or imaginary line is drawn outwards from that point at right angles. Next, 20 mm is located on the armour thickness scale and again a real or imagined line is drawn vertically upwards from it. As mentioned earlier, the intersection or crossing of these two lines is regarded as the point of impact as the round hits the target. In our example, it will be seen that the intersection is above the plot line and thus we can say that not surprisingly, our 40 mm round did indeed penetrate the 20 mm armour of the target.

Let us now consider something a bit beefier, with a 60 mm gun firing at a target which enjoys the protection of 90 mm armour. Again, we find the 60 mm gun on the vertical scale and come out at right angles. Moving to the armour thickness, 90 mm is found and the line followed vertically upwards. Where the two lines meet will be observed as being just below the line and so the shot is deemed not to have penetrated the target.

Using the armour penetration diagram, any calibre of gun up to 150 mm can fire at any thickness of armour up to 240 mm. It is accepted that the performance of the same calibre gun can vary depending on country of origin and so on, but once the basic idea behind the armour penetration diagram is understood, the more frequently used calibres and armour thicknesses encountered can be marked in by the wargamer for a faster reference. Further, the armour on a tank varies, depending on which part of the vehicle is in question. The PzKpfw VI Tiger 1 (H) for instance, had nose armour

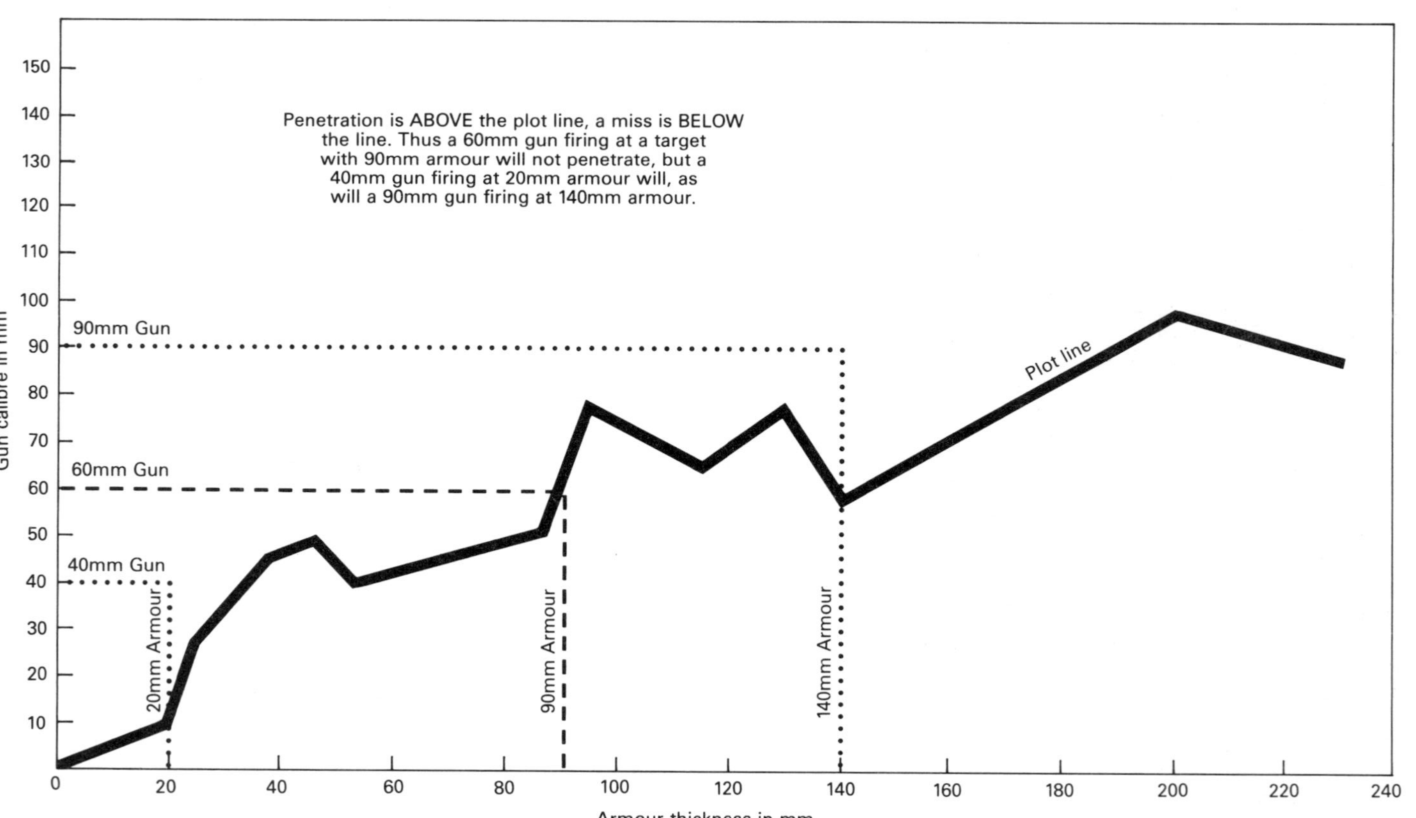

Gun calibre in mm
150
140
130
120
110
100
90
80
70
60
50
40
30
20
10
Penetration is ABOVE the plot line, a miss is BELOW
the line. Thus a 60mm gun firing at a target
with 90mm armour will not penetrate, but a
40mm gun firing at 20mm armour will, as
will a 90mm gun firing at 140mm armour.
90mm Gun
60mm Gun
40mm Gun
20mm Armour
90mm Armour
140mm Armour
Plot line
0
20
40
60
80
100
120
140
160
180
200
220
240
Armour thickness in mm

of 100 mm, lower side armour of 60 mm and the armour on the turret roof was 26 mm thick, so the effect of an anti-tank round is dependent on the part of the tank which it contacts. Using the diagram however, this is not a problem, for the required armour thickness is simply identified on the horizontal scale and the plot used in the manner described above. Thus any anti-tank gun can fire at any part of any tank—always provided that particular part of the tank is visible to the gunners and therefore vulnerable to attack. So, having established both the range and penetrative power of the anti-tank shell, there remains the question of the damage caused by a round hitting its target.

For the purposes of the present set of rules, it is sufficient to assume that a hit may still fail to contact a vulnerable spot and thus remain ineffective, or alternatively it could affect either the tank's engine or its gun. This can be rapidly summated by rolling one dice:

> 1–2 No effect
> 3–4 Hits on engine
> 5–6 Hits on gun

There is a differentiation with hits on the engine. If a '3' is scored, then the tank's engine is considered as being permanently damaged and beyond repair during the game. A '4' on the other hand gives the tank crew a chance to repair the damage, a task which will take the number of wargame moves indicated by rolling one dice. A tank with its engine permanently inoperative may, if the wargamer wishes, still fire its gun, but one which is having its engine repaired by the crew may not. It seems unlikely that the crew of a tank will have the necessary tools on board to carry out repairs to the gun, so no provision has been made for this within the context of the game. Since the engine is not effected, a tank with a gun which is out of service is best advised to make off for safety at high speed.

If the target is an armoured car or scout car, then it is much less likely to survive a direct hit. Once a hit has been registered in the manner described above, then the target is destroyed. Finally, it should be noted that anti-tank fire is effective only against armoured vehicles, not against infantry targets.

So there we have a basic set of rules by which some exciting World War II wargames can be conducted. It really doesn't matter what size figures are used, from 6 mm up to 54 mm, but wargamers working at the extreme ends of the scale may feel the need to modify the quoted distances. This will not affect the overall working of the rule mechanisms which have been constructed to apply equally well to any scale.

Advanced Rules

The above rules will provide for quite adequate games, but wargamers may wish to incorporate some additional aspects into the rules. The following paragraphs are suggestions for increasing the complexity of the rules and may be ignored or included, as required.

Hand Grenades

Hand grenades were frequently used in the war but, due to the ground scale, they can be difficult to portray in miniature. It is safe enough perhaps, to assume that a soldier is able to throw a grenade 50 yards, which equates to 50mm on the table top. We must, therefore, give the grenade a blast circle with a radius of less than 50mm. The light mortar was allocated one of 25mm, so one of 15mm for a grenade would be on the right lines. Any infantry in the open caught in the circle must have a 5 or 6 on one dice thrown for them to survive, whilst those in cover (this includes troops being transported in a vehicle, gun crews and so on) are only killed with a 6. Unarmoured vehicles will only be damaged with a 6. If they are so damaged, then the vehicles are out of action for the number of moves indicated by the roll of one dice. Hand grenades are judged to have no effect on armoured vehicles.

Flame-throwers

Something of an unsavoury weapon, the flame-thrower was used in different degrees by all the major participants of the war. In order to assess the potential of the flame-thrower, we can look at a couple of British weapons as examples. The man-portable version weighed 49 lbs, carried four gallons of fuel, could be fired no more than ten times and had a maximum range of 50 yards. A Churchill tank was modified to become a mobile flame-thrower (and as such was termed the "Crocodile") and towed a 6½-ton armoured trailer which contained 400 gallons of fuel. This fearsome weapon had a range of some 120 yards and could fire up to 80 one second bursts.

We can stipulate then that a man-carried flame-thrower has a

The Russian 76.2mm anti-tank gun, modelled here in 1/72 scale by Hinchliffe Models.

range of 50 mm, whilst one set in a tank can reach 120 mm. There is a case for limiting the number of times the weapon can fire during the game and it is suggested that the infantry version is restricted to three firings and the mobile to ten. As to the effect of the flame, well anything caught in its deadly path will be automatically lost, be it infantry in cover, the crew of a tank or whatever.

Communications

Essentially communication in the Second World War was by radio, although extensive use was still made of flag signalling in armoured formations, American, British and German tanks were all normally fitted with radios, but it took a while for the Russians to reach this stage. The radios in question were high frequency sets with a range of perhaps three or four miles, although this depended very much on the environment. It was a relatively simple procedure to establish radio contact—'netting in' as it was termed—and once contact was established it was usually successfully maintained. Given the relatively small area represented by the average wargames table, even when working in 1/300th scale, we can assume that all vehicles/units are in communication.

Morale

Wargamers generally set a lot of store by morale and many rule sets go into great depth on the subject. Within the context of some actions—an infantry/infantry confrontation for instance—morale may well be important, but it is likely to be less so within the framework of a fast moving and disjointed armoured action. Some fairly arbitrary rules can be used, such as specifying that one side must withdraw once a third of its strength has been either knocked out or killed, or something more complex can be introduced. The type of mechanism which can be used in this context is to delay the response of a unit to written orders if the morale of that unit is seen to be questionable. Alternatively, the unit may not be permitted to take offensive action—this includes firing—until it is once more in good order. The reasons and causes for morale tests are many, but they can be grouped under such headings as casualties, dispersal and so on. Basically, the wargamer is free to include as many morale limitations as is seen fit, or to omit morale completely.

Ammunition Restrictions

There was a finite limit to the amount of ammunition that could be carried into battle. We have seen earlier how tank crews waived any safety regulations in order to carry extra rounds and the infantry engaged in similar activities, although to a lesser degree, for they still had to bodily carry the extra ammunition. With an infantryman

A Nitto 1/72 scale plastic kit of the German rocket firing Nebelwerfer.

on average carrying between 60 and 80 rounds for his rifle and a tank equipped typically with 100 rounds, there is little argument for units running completely out of ammunition during a wargame. It is accepted that there are exceptions to this, particularly when one talks about self-propelled guns—the German Hummel with 18 rounds or the Italian Semovente 90/53 with six, for example—but generally the argument holds true. What can happen, however, is that the tank, rather than the infantryman, runs out of the correct type of ammunition. The average tank carried three types of ammunition, armour piercing, high explosive and smoke. Sources are vague as to the exact proportion of each type, leading to the conclusion that it would be left to the discretion of the local commanders to decide, probably dependent on the type of operation being planned.

In a similar manner, the wargamer can decide how much of each ammunition type the miniature tanks will carry. As an example, we could allow a wargame tank to carry, say, 20 rounds of ammunition, which would be more than sufficient to see it through an average wargame encounter. The ammunition in our example is composed of 12 rounds armour piercing, six of high explosive and two of smoke. A record is kept of the tank's ammunition expenditure and the type of round fired. As the wargame progresses, the situation may arise that our tank has nine rounds left—in other words, just under half its total ammunition quota—but only one of those rounds is armour piercing, since the tank has either not needed, or had the opportunity, to fire the high explosive or smoke rounds. This type of situation can impose problems on the wargame general, who will need to decide whether to withdraw this vehicle from the engagement, or trust to luck and place its last armour piercing round in the breech.

In a generalised set of rules such as these, full coverage cannot be given to every aspect of warfare and the wargamer is encouraged to create 'local' mechanisms and rules to cover the varying situations as they occur on the table top. Problems such as commando raids, paratroop drops, glider-borne troops, partisan/resistance activities, minefields and the clearance of same, are just a few examples of the fascinating mechanisms which can be explored and included within the overall framework of the wargame.

Scenarios

Having organised the rules, we can now look at their use in some fairly typical wargames scenarios. With only a finite amount of space, the choice of scenario is limited and, as a result, only the more popular theatres of the war are covered. I was tempted to aim for the more off-beat type of wargame, say with Greek guerillas fighting some second rate Italian troops, or looking at the Allied advance into Ethiopia in 1941. Interestingly enough, however, there is a surprising lack of wargames material for these sideshows and I felt that it would be more than a little unkind to inspire the wargamer with scenarios, only for them to find that the kit needed to play out the game was not available. Thus, only situations for which there is a good supply of figures and vehicles have been selected.

Even here there are problems, for the inclusion of all the major powers—Germany, Italy and Japan v. France, Russia, United Kingdom and the United States—in smaller situations is tricky. The scenarios are designed as being suitable for any and all scales of figures, from 6 mm to 54 mm. Any remarks as to one scale being more suitable than another are included within the introduction of the relevant scenario. The intention is to make the situations both increasingly complicated and varying in concept as a wider variety of weapons is introduced. In reality the number of wargame situations offered by World War II is virtually without limit. Whether it is a small action that is required or a major offensive, there is a wide choice of situations from which to choose. From the desperate struggles around the ever-decreasing perimeter of Dunkirk to the snow-covered slopes of Norway, from the mountainous Greek countryside to the heat of the North African desert or the Middle East, from the grandiose sweep of the Eastern Front to the relative confines of Normandy, there is indeed a rich choice of scenario.

Down in the Jungle...

It is late 1942 and the setting is the hinterland of one of the innumerable small islands which make up the Solomons chain. An invading Japanese task force of approximately regimental strength has become bogged down and is being counter-attacked by American and Australian troops.

We can assume that the Japanese will have lost some of their number, but essentially a unit of regimental strength would muster

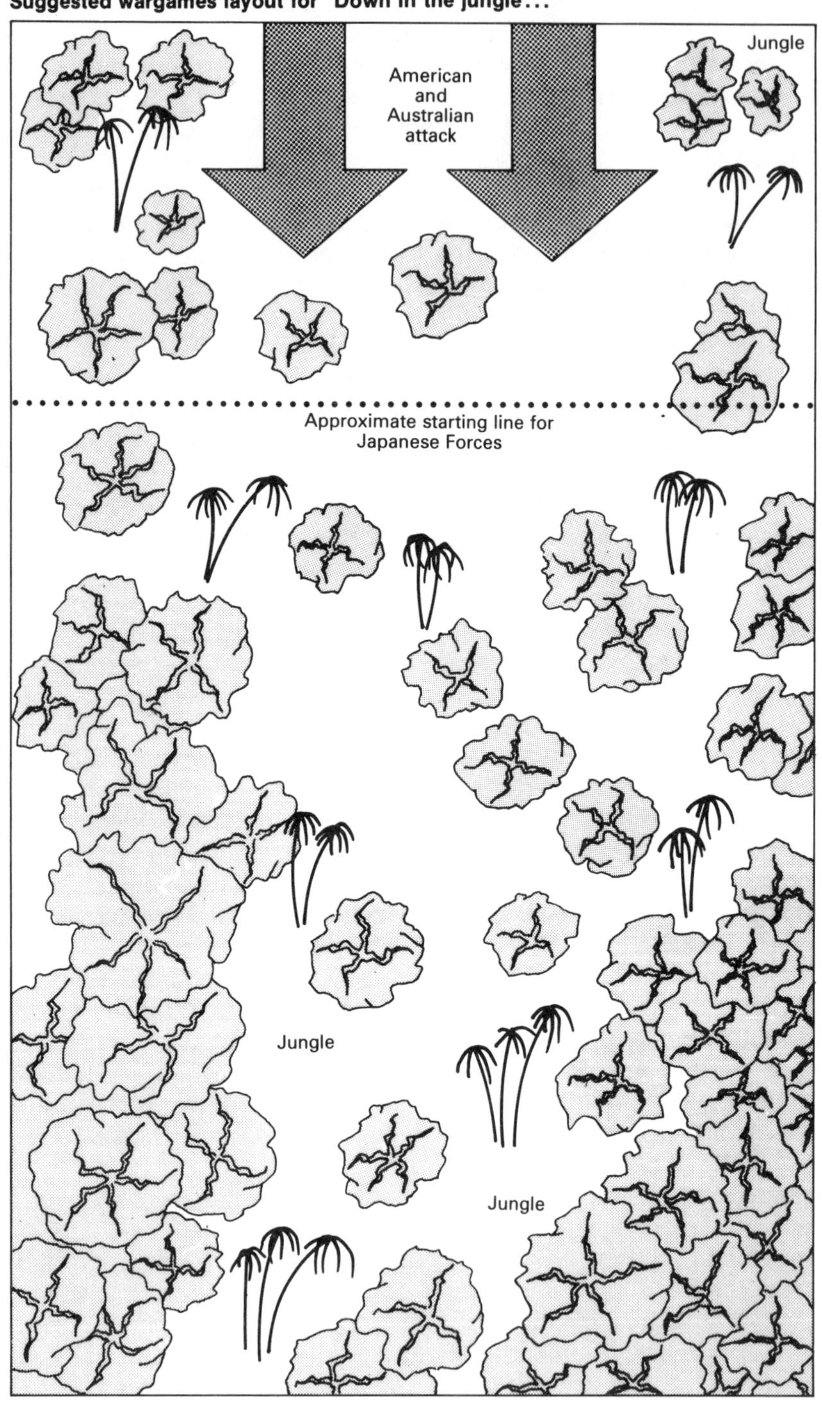
Jungle
American
and
Australian
attack
Approximate starting line for
Japanese Forces
Jungle
Jungle

perhaps 800 men. Typically the men could be from the Japanese version of marines, the Special Naval Landing Force or ordinary infantry. The Japanese seemed to specialise in *ad hoc* formations and any troops in a particular area could be rounded up for a specific mission. This gives the wargamer a great deal of leeway either to mix up the Japanese forces or to field a more specialised formation. If the wargamer wishes, this scenario can be fought as a regimental-sized action, but the intention is to depict one of, say, infantry company size—60 men divided into six platoons each of eight men and a platoon headquarters of 12 men. In this situation, the figure/man ratio could conceivably be 1:1, for 60 figures are easy enough to handle on the table top. The lowest ratio which could be used is 1:5, requiring 12 wargames figures, but this would tend to reduce the effect and impact of the battle. Again, if desired, the platoon rather than the company could be considered as being the basic unit on which the game is based, thereby reducing the number of figures required, but this does tend to make the game a skirmish. Assuming, then, a company action, the Japanese forces would have 53 men with rifles, six with lmgs and maybe a 50mm mortar. It is unlikely that any heavier weapons would come into play at this level and so it is an all-infantry combat that is under consideration.

The Australian troops could, for the sake of balance, be considered as consisting of a weak company of three platoons, 30 men in all, 24 of whom are equipped with rifles, three with smgs and three with lmgs. Alongside the Australians are the Americans, whose forces are a full-strength company of 43 men from the Marine Corps. This gives the Americans quite an impressive array of firepower—18 rifles, eight Browning Automatic Rifles (BAR), six smgs, two flame-throwers and a bazooka. Thus the Allied forces muster 73 men to the Japanese 60 and the balance of firepower is also in their favour.

The terrain is basically that of a jungle island interior, with as much foliage as the wargamer feels able to handle, or rather deploy, on the wargames table. A balance between realism and playability has to be found here, for model soldiers do have to be moved around and it's a little tiresome if trees keep falling over every few minutes. One solution is to place one or two symbolic trees on suitably coloured pieces of felt or card and count all the area covered by the material to be jungle. Although visually less pleasing, this method does permit the movement of troops. Possibly an ideal answer would be to fill the edges and corners of the wargames table with trees and use the representative method in the centre, where, presumably, most of the action will take place. Prepared defensive positions are not a part of this scenario, which is intended to portray a somewhat disorganised chance encounter in the interior of a nameless island. A few rocks and some clumps of the ever useful lichen scattered over the table will suffice to represent undergrowth.

The Japanese troops are deployed about two-thirds of the way across the table, with the Allies coming on at the edge nearest to them. For the Japanese player, the scenario can be won by the Japanese infantry successfully withdrawing to the far edge of the table, while the Allied player wins if this is prevented from happening. In the final analysis, degrees of victory are not really possible—if the Japanese forces do not reach the 'distant' edge of the table, they have lost. This may be considered as being too hard and fast by some wargamers and there are a couple of mechanisms which could be introduced to offer some degree of success. Casualties could come into the reckoning, for the Japanese cannot really claim a victory if only one surviving infantryman makes it safely to the edge. The Allies can be considered as fighting down to two-thirds strength, i.e. suffering from one third of their number as casualties before they will break off the action, whereas the Japanese can fight down to one third, i.e. lose two thirds of their men, before they are considered as out of the fight. One reads of the fanatical defensive properties of the Japanese soldier, but the 'last-man-alive' type of game does not really make for an interesting encounter. However, should the wargamer wish to introduce this into the scenario there should be no real problem, but local morale rules may have to be drawn up.

Equally, a limit can be placed on the duration of the game, if the Japanese do not reach the 'home' table edge in a given number of moves, then the Allies have won. The same stricture cannot, however, be placed on the Allies, for they were already on the island and seek only to drive the encroaching Japanese from same. One method of calculating the number of moves to allow is to reckon the total number of moves that it would take the Japanese to reach the table edge unhindered and then add 50%. Thus, if it would take them ten moves to reach safety unimpeded by the attention of the Allies, allow them 15 moves in the game situation.

This type of scenario, realistically free of armoured vehicles, allows the wargamer to examine and explore the role of the infantryman in action. The ranges of the weapons involved will be severely curtailed by limitations imposed by the terrain, and players will need to be conscientious when checking lines of sight. Although not listed in the weaponry, it seems reasonable to allow both sides a number of hand grenades and pistols. The amount and allocation of these can be left to the discretion of the wargamer, but I suggest that this is not overdone. Perhaps 20 hand grenades and six to eight pistols a side would be sufficient. Ammunition restrictions do not really apply in this type of scenario, for each man would carry a fair amount. The Japanese mortar could be allocated a limited number of bombs but, in practice, the Japanese player will find that the mortar is a distinct encumbrance in such a fast-moving game and could do well to abandon it at the outset. If a figure is required, I suggest that an allowance of six mortar bombs will be about right.

This Sand Gets Everywhere...

For this scenario we are in the Western Desert in 1942. In early November of that year, during the Battle of El Alamein, the Italian Ariete Armoured Group clashed with the British 7th Armoured Division to the south-east of that town. While it is not the intention to fully recreate this campaign, the scenario depicts a typical action set against the background of that engagement. The two opposing forces meet in open terrain in an essentially fluid encounter battle in which every tank or gun is treated as an individual unit to move and/or fire as the situation permits.

The Italian Armoured Group was a mix of a number of different units which, in essence, were as follows: 52nd Tank Battalion, 3rd Nizza Armoured Group (armoured Bersaglieri with a/t and a/a batteries), 132nd Tank Regiment (8th, 9th and 10th Tank Battalions), 8th Bersaglieri Regiment (2nd motor cycle battalion, 5th and 12th motorised battalion), 132nd Armoured Artillery Regiment (1st and 2nd 75/27 groups, 3rd 105/28 group, 551 and 552 75/18 armoured groups) and the 4th Granatieri di Sardegna (Sardinian Grenadiers) Anti-tank Battalion. Surely there is something for everyone there! The main tank was the M13/40, but a mix of any of the Italian tanks which were used is quite permissible. This adds to the appearance of the game and makes the amassing of the necessary vehicles that bit more interesting. It is not always advantageous to go for the heaviest, latest and best weapon of the period. This approach, apart from being historically both inaccurate and unrepresentative, will be found to be very limiting and tedious. It is far better to try to represent an accurate mix of weapons and vehicles even with all the inherent problems this may cause. One's wargaming will be that much more enjoyable and interesting as a result, and a good deal more satisfaction will be gained from using a balanced, historically accurate army.

On an average size wargames table, it will be found that a dozen or so tanks, half as many anti-tank guns and perhaps a couple of self-propelled guns, will provide a sufficient force for an enjoyable action. The field artillery and infantry components have been omitted from this scenario, which is intended to be in the nature of a mobile armoured engagement, but they can be included if the wargamer so wishes, as can some armoured cars. Although I suggest that the wargamer working in the 1/72, 1/76 or 1/200 scale

Suggested wargames layout for 'this sand gets everywhere...'

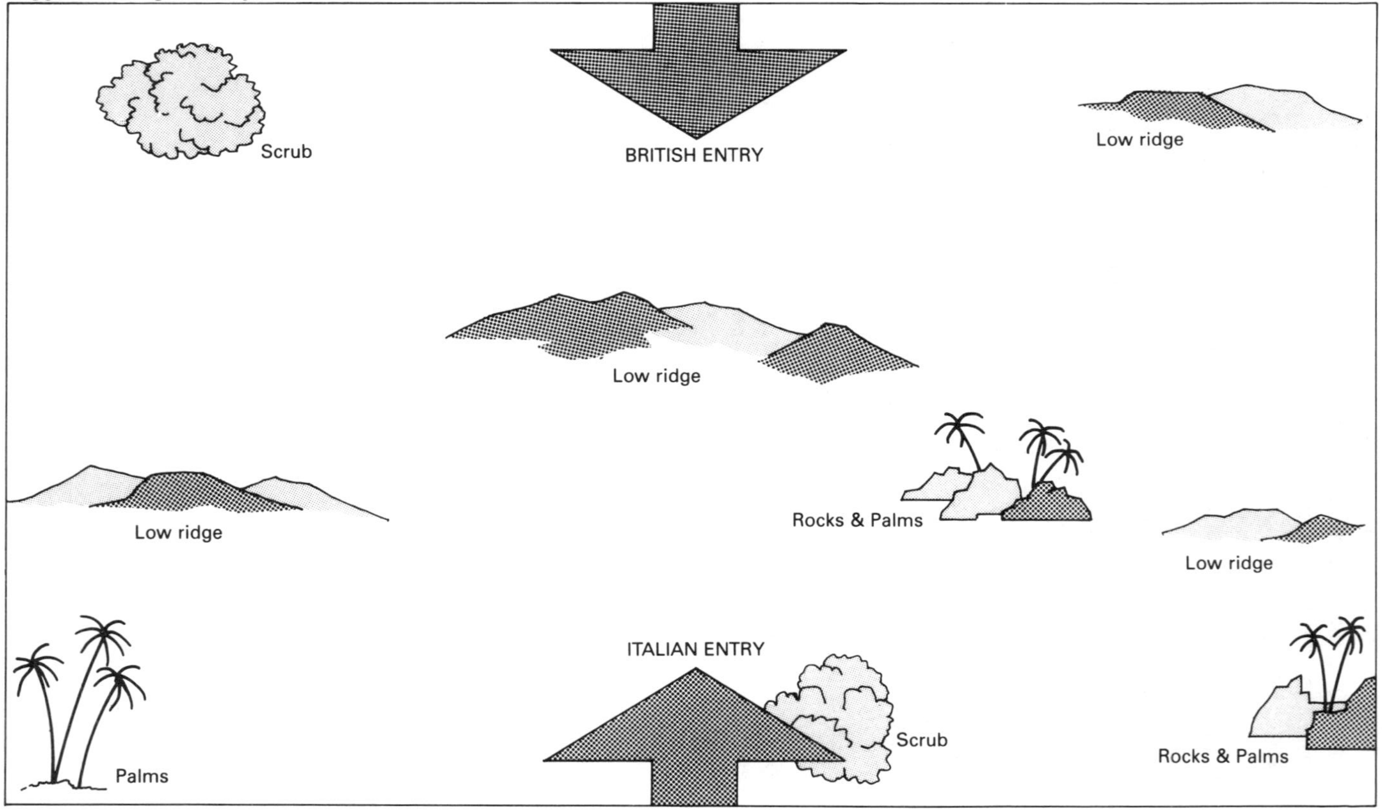

fields this, or a similar, representative mix of tanks, self-propelled artillery and towed anti-tank guns rather than the complete division, in 1/300 scale it would be quite feasible to portray the entire formation, if so required.

After being formed as the Mobile Division, Egypt in 1938, the 7th Armoured Division took that name in April 1940. By 1942 the Division consisted of two armoured brigades, the 4th (Royal Scots Greys, 4/8th Hussars in tanks, 2nd Derbyshire Yeomanry (armoured cars), 3rd RHA (25 pdrs) and the 1st Bn Kings Royal Rifle Corps) and the 22nd (1st RTR, 5th RTR, 4th City of London Yeomanry in tanks, 4th and 97th Field Regiments Royal Artillery (25 pdrs) and the 1st Bn The Rifle Brigade), supported by the 131st infantry brigade (3 bns of infantry from the Queen's Regiment, 53rd Field Regiment Royal Artillery and two anti-tank formations), and a number of divisional units such as the 11th Hussars equipped with armoured cars and the 65th Anti-Tank Regiment, Royal Artillery who had 6 pdrs.

At the time of the battle, the four armoured regiments which made up the British 7th Armoured Division were equipped with Crusader, Grant and Stuart tanks. These were supported by an armoured car regiment, four 25 pdrs regiments, several batteries of 6 pdr anti-tank guns and three battalions of infantry carried in lorries. Once again, I suggest that a selection of tanks is used—as a guide, there were twice as many Grants as there were of the other two types, so wargamers may wish to reflect this in their table top forces. There is no reason why the British cannot field a similar number of tanks and field or anti-tank guns as the Italians.

The terrain for this scenario should be as open as possible. That said, the real desert does not always conform to the popular 'sea of sand' concept, so it would be useful if the table top variety didn't either. A few very low ridges, some date palms and perhaps a few rocks sparsely decorated with small amounts of lichen will serve to alleviate the overall barrenness and still maintain an open playing area. If the players wish, some of the anti-tank guns can be 'dug-in' in prepared positions, hoping that the enemy's tanks will come into their sights. Such positions can be re-enforced by sandbags or some other temporary defensive work.

The intended essence of this scenario is its fluidity, with tanks swirling around the table top, each attempting to out-manoeuvre the enemy vehicles. It really should be a survival of the fittest, but there should be a figure at which one side will seek to break contact. A rule could be drawn up to stipulate that when 50% of the tanks of either side are out of commission, for whatever reason, then that side must withdraw from the conflict. Alternatively, points could be awarded for each enemy vehicle damaged, disabled or knocked out. The game could be set to last for a certain number of moves and at the end, the points total for each side assessed. The simplistic outcome is that the player with the most points for damage inflicted on the enemy is the winner, but his own force must still be over 50% strong to qualify for victory.

Struggle in the Suburbs...

We move on now to April 1945, the last year of the war. The scene is the eastern suburbs of Berlin, where the German defenders are prepared for a final stand against the encroaching Russians under Marshal Zhukov.

The German forces are a mixture of civilians and soldiers of all age groups. Men from units which have ceased to exist fight alongside the fanatical diehards, while veterans of the Great War once more lift a rifle in anger as members of the Hitler Youth find themselves under fire. Scattered elements of the much vaunted Panzer formations provide supporting fire with their heavy tanks—powerful enough, but far too few in number. Resolved to sell their lives dearly and to contest every yard of ground, these mismatched German forces provide the Russians with ferocious resistance. In terms of a wargames force it really is a case of "anything goes" for this particular scenario. Some suitably armed civilian figures, soldiers from all arms of the services, sailors, members of the Luftwaffe, paratroopers, Waffen SS, the SS themselves—all will fit the bill here. The actual number of figures used depends on the space available, but on the average sized wargames table it will be found that between 60 and 80 figures can be satisfactorily deployed. Some six or seven tanks can be used, all of them heavy—Tiger I and IIs and perhaps Panthers—along with a good number of anti-tank guns of all calibres and possibly a couple of field guns. The foot figures, in addition to the usual rifles and machine guns, could be armed with hand-held anti-tank weapons, petrol bombs and so forth.

For their part the Russians can field as many men and armoured fighting vehicles as can realistically be placed on the wargames table. From 1944, each of the nine tank battalions of a Russian Tank Corps fielded 21 T-34 tanks, so the wargamer is not restricted in any historical sense. The motorised infantry element of the same Corps had three battalions, each approximately 600 men strong, whilst there were also anti-tank units, self-propelled artillery regiments, mortar regiments and a heavy tank regiment, this latter possibly being equipped with the JS-I tank. If all this represents rather too much armour for the wargamer's taste, then elements of a Russian Rifle Division with armoured support could be represented instead but, that said, it was the tank formations which the Russians used in their assault on Berlin. In practical terms, much will depend on the wargamer's resources, but a dozen or so tanks, supported by a

Suggested wargames layout for "Struggle in the suburbs..."

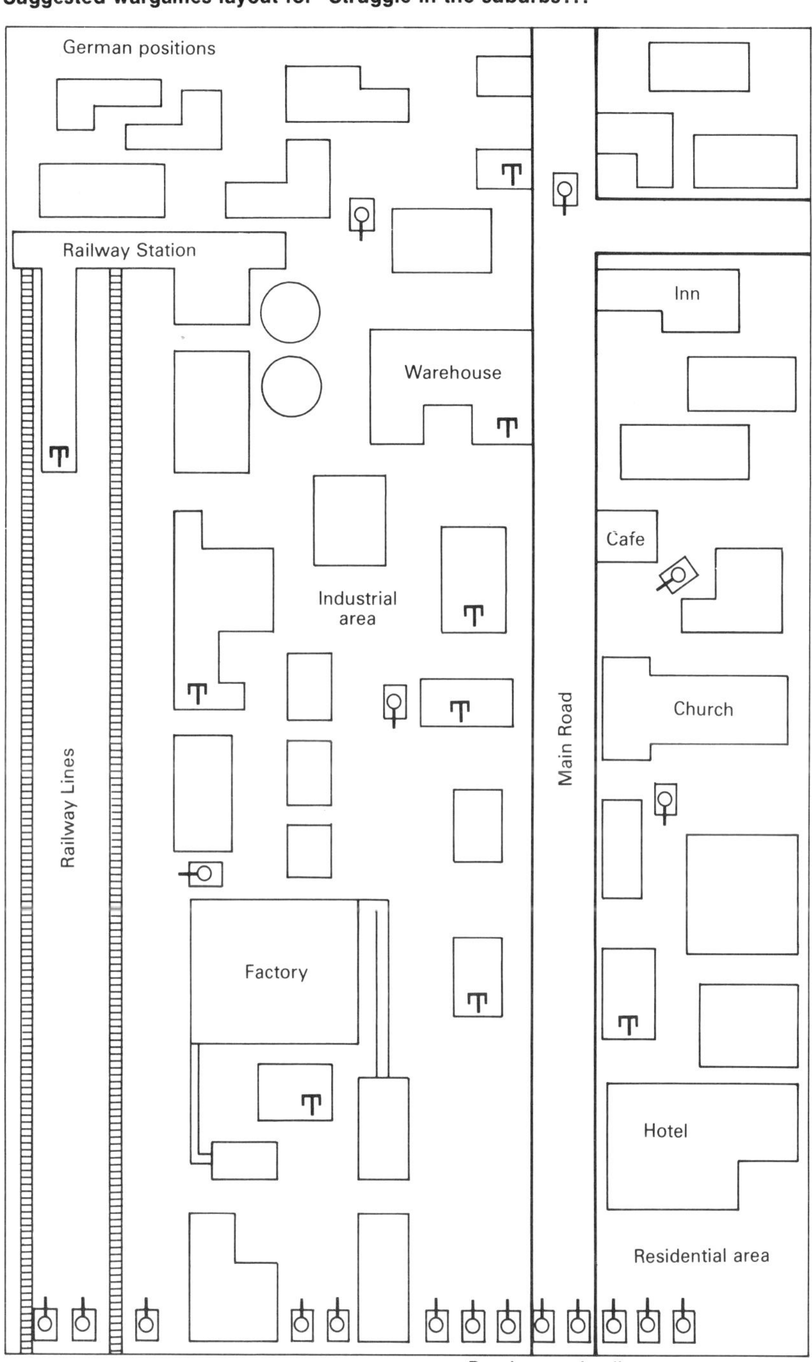

= Anti-Tank gun

lesser number of self-propelled guns and perhaps 30 to 40 infantry would look the part whilst still remaining reasonably controllable.

The terrain for this particular scenario can be as complex or as simple as the wargamer requires. Ruined buildings—factories, houses, offices and shops—can appear in numbers; railway lines, stations and so forth are all suitable. It is to the distinct advantage of the German defenders to have as many ruined buildings and as much 'rubble' as possible depicted on the table. Not only will such scenery provide innumerable defensive positions for the Germans, the Russian progress will also be impeded as they seek to find a way across the table top.

The mechanism of this confrontation is of the static defence—there was nowhere else left for the defenders to go—being assailed by superior numbers and firepower. The task of the Russian commander is to fight his way across the table top in what must be a set number of moves. Indeed, in order to reflect the westwards push for the taking of Berlin, the only victory condition available to the Russians is this possession of ground. For their part, the Germans can have one of two victory conditions. Given that the Russians are allotted a fixed number of moves in which to cross the table top, the Germans win if this is not achieved. Secondly, each Russian tank, gun and infantryman is given a points value (the actual value in itself is irrelevant, it simply serves to supply a numerical total). As the Germans take out a tank or whatever, the points value of that piece is logged and an accumulative total is noted. Should this total reach a pre-determined figure before the Russians reach the far table edge, then the German defenders are deemed to have won the game.

Inevitably, given the constantly changing nature of wargaming, any information regarding the availability of 'kit' which is given in print will date very quickly. New figure manufacturers come into the hobby fairly frequently and established manufacturers are constantly producing new releases. New books and rule sets are continually published while others are either remaindered or go out of print, and thus the hobby is in a perpetual state of flux. That said, the reader generally expects to find some indication as to what is currently in the market place and the following comments are provided in an attempt to fulfil this requirement.

Figures and Vehicle Kits

In the following listing, 20 mm, which strictly speaking is equivalent to 1/87 scale, has been taken as relating to the 1/76 and 1/72 scales. Whilst realising this is not quite accurate, I plead common usage.
Acropolis (Scotia Enterprises, 32, West Hemming Street, Letham, Angus DD8 2PU). Under their "Warsquad" label, this company offer a range of 20 mm (1/72) white metal infantry figures.

Action 200 (Skytrex Ltd, 28, Brook Street, Wymeswold, Loughborough, Leics.). A rapidly growing range of 9 mm (1/200) scale figures and equipment in white metal.

Airfix

The first manufacturer to produce 20 mm (1/72 scale) soft plastic soldiers and hard plastic vehicle kits, this company has, or rather had, an extensive WWII range. Finding all the various releases can be a work of art however, for the boxes seem to suffer from an extremely erratic production schedule. The figures and vehicles are worth a search, for they are reasonably priced and still, in spite of the age of the moulds, well detailed. The company also manufacture a much more limited range of 54 mm (1/32) figures and even fewer vehicles, again in soft plastic.
Cromwell Models (Regency House, 22, Hayburn Street, Glasgow G11

6DG). This company produces an extensive range of 20 mm (1/76) polyurethane plastic resin tank and vehicle kits which offer excellent detail.

Esci

Another manufacturer of 20 mm (1/72) plastic figures, with an extensive, well-modelled and useful range, all of which is available at the time of writing.

Fujimi (1/72)/Nitto (1/76)

These two manufacturers of plastic vehicle kits recently joined forces. Their combined output is, as a result, considerable and they offer an excellent variety which includes some unusual items. Note though that whilst Fujimi are 1/72 scale, Nitto are marginally smaller at 1/76.

Hasegawa

Provides a range of 20 mm (1/72) plastic kits of tanks and unarmoured vehicles.

Hinchliffe Models (Skytrex Ltd, 28, Brook Street, Wymeswold, Loughborough, Leics.). An extremely comprehensive range of 20 mm (1/72) infantry, guns, tanks and other vehicles in white metal. With new releases being constantly added, this range is continually expanding.

Matchbox

Matchbox offer a modest range of 20 mm (1/72) plastic kits of tanks and other military vehicles, along with several boxes of soft plastic figures in the same scale.

MLR Figures (111, Greere Road, London E15 3PP). A relatively new manufacturer, producing some finely detailed white metal figures in 20 mm (1/72).

Platoon 20 (Model Figures & Hobbies, Lower Balloo Road, Groomsport, County Down BT19 2LU, Northern Ireland). An extremely comprehensive range of 20 mm (1/72) white metal figures in a variety of equipment, kit and poses.

Scotia Micromodels (32, West Hemming Street, Letham, Angus DD8 2PU.). This company produce a useful range of 6 mm (1/300) tanks and other vehicles in white metal.

Skytrex Ltd (28, Brook Street, Wymeswold, Loughborough, Leics.). Produce an interesting range of 3 mm (1/600) beach assault equipment in white metal. As yet limited in scope, this range offers great promise.

Tradition (5a, Shepherd Street, Mayfair, London W1). A limited range of 30 mm (1/58) white metal infantry.

Wild Geese Miniatures (71, Daneland, East Barnet, Herts EN4 8PZ). A relatively new manufacturer producing 9 mm (1/200) vehicles and infantry in white metal.

Scenery

Hovels (18, Glebe Road, Scartho, Grimsby, South Humberside DN33 2HL). Hovels produce some interesting resin cast buildings in a well established 15 mm (1/120) range and latterly in 6 mm (1/300).

Rules

Newbury Rules (15, Cromwell Road, Shaw, Newbury, Berkshire). Cambrai to Sinai.

Tabletop Games (53, Mansfield Road, Daybrook, Nottingham NG5 6BB). Combined Arms (1/300), Tactical Commander, Firefly (1/300).

Wargames Research Group (The Keep, Le Marchant Barracks, London Road, Devizes, Wiltshire SN10 2ER). 1925–50 Infantry-Armour Rules.

General Books

The amount of books available on World War II is prodigious and defies any summary. Some of the best books are those that are out of print and yet fairly shallow publications of the 'coffee table' standard seem always to be with us. The list that follows is no more than a précis of some of the books which I found to be both interesting and informative.

Belfield E. & H. Essame *The Battle For Normandy* Batsford 1965

Buckland R. *Military Modelling Guide to Military Vehicles* Argus Books 1988

Chamberlain P. & Ellis C. *British & American Tanks of World War II* Arms & Armour Press 1969

Chamberlain P. & Ellis C. *Pictorial History of the Tanks of the World* Arms & Armour Press 1972

Chamberlain P. & Gander T. *Allied Pistols, Rifles & Grenades* 1976

Chamberlain P. & Gander T. *Axis Pistols, Rifles & Grenades* 1976

Chamberlain P. & Gander T. *Infantry, Mountain & Airborne Guns* 1975

Chamberlain P. & Gander T. *Machine Guns* 1974

Chamberlain P. & Gander T. *Mortars & Rockets* 1975

Chamberlain P. & Gander T. *Sub-machine Guns & Automatic Rifles* (Macdonald and Jane's *WW2 Fact Files* Series) 1976

Crow D. *British & Commonwealth Armoured Formations 1919–46* Profile Publications Ltd 1971

Doyle H. & Kliment C. *Czechoslovak Armoured Fighting Vehicles 1918–1945* Bellona 1979

Dunnigan J. (ed) *The Russian Front: Germany's War in the East 1941–45* Arms & Armour Press 1978

Gander T. & Chamberlain P. *American Tanks of World War 2* PSL 1977

Gander T. & Chamberlain P. *British Tanks of World War 2* PSL 1976
Gander T. & Chamberlain P. *German Tanks of World War 2* PSL 1975
Hogg I. *The Illustrated Encyclopaedia of Artillery* Guild Publishing 1987
Hogg I. & Weeks J. *The Illustrated Encyclopedia of Military Vehicles* Prentice-Hall 1980
Jones M. *Guide to Military Modelling* Argus Books 1987
Natkeil R. *War Maps: Campaigns & Battles of World War II* Bison 1985
RAC Tank Museum *Fire & Movement* 1975
Riccio R. *Italian Tanks & Fighting Vehicles of World War 2* Pique Publications 1975
Senger, von & Etterlin *German Tanks of World War II* Arms & Armour Press 1969
Urquhart Major Gen. *Arnhem* Cassell & Co Ltd 1958
Wise T. *D-Day to Berlin* Arms & Armour Press 1979
Werner M. *The Military Strength of the Great Powers* Victor Gollancz 1939

Mention should also be made of the excellent Men-At-Arms and Vanguard series of books which are published by Osprey. Concise, informative and containing numerous black and white illustrations in addition to full colour artwork, these titles – too numerous to name here – are splendid value for money.

Wargaming Books

Asquith, S. *Guide to Wargaming* Argus Books 1987
Asquith, S. *Guide to Solo Wargaming* Argus Books 1988
Featherstone D. *Wargaming Airborne Operations* Kaye & Ward 1977
Featherstone D. *Wargames Through the Ages Vol. 4 1861–1945* Stanley Paul 1976
Featherstone D. *Featherstone's Complete Wargaming* David & Charles 1988
Featherstone D. & Robinson K. *Battles with Model Tanks* Macdonald & Jane's 1979
Shaw I. *WWII Army Organisations & Equipment* Tabletop Games 1986
Wise T. *Battles for Wargamers World War II Tunisia* Bellona 1973
Wise T. *Battles for Wargamers World War II The Western Desert* Bellona 1972

All the above titles should be available from local libraries, but two reputable and recommended bookshops are:

Athena Books, 34, Imperial Crescent, Town Moor, Doncaster, South Yorkshire DN2 5BU

W.E. Hersant Ltd, 228, Archway Road, London N6 5AZ

Section II–The War at Sea

5   *Organisation*

When dealing with the navies of the various countries, one cannot really discuss organisation in the accepted sense of the word. The formations adopted were very fluid, with task forces being assembled for a particular mission and then disbanded, convoy escorts being arranged, and so on. There were exceptions of course, The Royal Navy's Force H for example, which consisted chiefly of the aircraft carrier *Ark Royal*, the battle cruiser *Renown* and the cruiser *Sheffield*, was together for the best part of three years from 1940 to 1943. Another example could be Force Z—the battleship *Prince of Wales* and the battle cruiser *Repulse*—although this did not serve very long before being sunk by the Japanese in 1941. Each warship was its own formation and was usually quite capable of operating both as a single unit or as an essentially independent element of a larger force.

With this in mind, the following generalised remarks are intended to offer the wargamer some idea as to the comparative strengths of the various navies involved in the Second World War, rather than to examine fleet or flotilla organisation in some detail.

The French Navy
At the outbreak of war, the French Navy had three battleships, two battle cruisers, an aircraft carrier, a seaplane carrier, 15 cruisers, 75 destroyers and 59 submarines on active deployment. The largest concentration of warships was in the Mediterranean to counter the threat posed by the Italian fleet.

As France fell, the French Navy moved its warships to ports in North Africa, but the Vichy Government could only retain them if these ships came under German or Italian control. This required the vessels to be moved to the naval base at Toulon where most of them were scuttled in late 1942 as the Germans, having ended Vichy France, neared the port. A number of French warships had sailed to England and were taken over by the Royal Navy. Some Vichy units in the port of Mers el Kebir were attacked by the Royal Navy to prevent them fighting for the Axis powers, a move which upset the French naval personnel in England. Initially lacking in capital ships due to these various actions, the Free French Navy as a result was rarely more than a token force throughout the early years of the war.

In the early war period the French Fleet Air Arm had 350 aircraft, all of which were shore-based and organised as four squadrons of dive bombers, two of seaplanes and one of flying boats.

The German Navy

The German Navy was organised into three divisions or commands —capital ships, submarines and the other types of warships and auxiliaries. At the outbreak of war Germany had three pocket battleships, two battle cruisers, three heavy cruisers, six light cruisers, 22 destroyers, 20 torpedo boats, 59 submarines and two old pre-Dreadnought battleships. More pocket battleships and heavy cruisers were built however and the Navy expanded rapidly. Many of these units were soon stationed in the Baltic under Admiral Albrecht who commanded the two elderly battleships, three destroyers, nine torpedo boats, two of the light cruisers and eight mine-layers. The Battle of the Atlantic has been discussed earlier in this book. The main German deployment in this particular theatre was of submarines, with occasionally, capital ships. The German surface raiders and submarines were a constant menace to Allied shipping, as were the converted merchantmen, which Germany used with great success. Eventually all the German pocket battleships were either sunk or disabled and, at the end of the war, the German Navy had only three cruisers and 12 destroyers left.

The Germans did not possess a Fleet Air Arm, instead a Luftwaffe officer was allocated to the Naval High Command and it was his task to organise any airpower the Navy might need from Luftwaffe squadrons.

The Italian Navy

The Italian Navy possessed four battleships, eight heavy and 14 light cruisers, 128 destroyers, 115 submarines and 62 torpedo boats. Its apparent strength is misleading though, for the Italian Navy always held the Royal Navy in awe and, as a result, never performed very well in the Mediterranean, an area it could well have dominated following the sudden demise of the French Navy. One area where it did do well was in the use of fast, light attack craft armed either with torpedoes for attacking shipping or geared up as anti-submarine boats. The Italians had considerable success using these craft, badly damaging the Royal Navy's battleships *Queen Elizabeth* and *Valiant* as well as the cruiser *HMS York*. Once the Italians dropped

The battleship HMS _Ramillies_ in May 1943. Notice the false bow painted on to confuse enemy submarines.

out of the war in late 1943, those ships which avoided German seizure made for Allied ports and surrendered.

Like the Germans, the Italian Navy relied on the air force for its air cover.

The Japanese Navy

The Japanese Navy came under the heading of The Combined Fleet, which was sub-divided into seven smaller fleets, all of which mustered ten aircraft carriers, a like number of battleships, four seaplane carriers, 39 cruisers, 74 destroyers, eight minelayers, 13 escorts and 63 submarines. This force was supported by a number of auxiliary craft located at a number of bases. Task forces were composed of ships drawn from any and all of the seven fleets and within them, groups of small warships were always led by a larger vessel. In the destroyers, four ships made up a division and four divisions a squadron to which a cruiser was attached as the leader.

The Japanese Navy had its own air arm operating from the Fleet aircraft carriers and its own Naval Land Forces who functioned to all intents and purposes as marines.

The Royal Navy

The most powerful navy in the world in 1939, the Royal Navy operating from the UK was deployed in three main sections. The Home Fleet was based on two aircraft carriers, seven battleships and battle cruisers and 15 cruisers. The North Atlantic was covered by two cruisers with attendant vessels, while two aircraft carriers, a like number of battleships and five cruisers were retained in home ports with responsibilities for escort, patrol and attack missions. The larger ships, i.e. down to and including cruisers, were grouped into units of between two and nine ships, but the smaller vessels were organised into flotillas, typically of eight ships.

The Mediterranean saw the Navy committed to the defence of the islands of Gibraltar and Malta, as well as the Suez Canal. The Mediterranean Fleet based at Alexandria consisted, at the outbreak of war, of three battleships, an aircraft carrier, six cruisers and a number of smaller vessels. With the demise of the French Navy and the Italian declaration of war, the Navy's resources were stretched, but reinforcements were sent when possible, until by late 1943 there were six battleships, two aircraft carriers and ten cruisers. The loss of Singapore, as well as that of *HMS Prince of Wales* and *HMS Repulse* effectively prevented the Royal Navy from becoming involved in the Pacific naval war until well towards the end. By early 1945, however, the Pacific Fleet was based at Sydney and mustered a battleship, four aircraft carriers, three cruisers and ten destroyers.

The North Atlantic was the scene of bitter fighting throughout the war. As well as blockading German ports, the Navy had to keep the supply lanes to the British Isles open and protected. The German capital ships *Graf Spee*, *Bismarck*, *Scharnhorst* and *Tirpitz* were all sunk and eventually the German submarine menace was countered and overcome. As a direct result of the Navy's efforts, the D-Day landings took place free of interference from the German Navy.

Before leaving this section, mention should also be made here of the Australian and New Zealand Navies who fought alongside Royal Navy units, often with their crews brought up to strength by British sailors.

The Royal Marines were the Navy's own soldiers and from them were formed a number of the élite Commando formations. The organisation of Commando units varied, but a typical outfit might consist of a headquarters and three troops, each 30 strong and further divided into three sections.

The Fleet Air Arm started the war with just under 200 aircraft

HMS *Broadway*, an ex-American 'four stacker' in British service.

operating from aircraft carriers and seaplane carriers. There were also a number of spotter planes, but these were operated from catapults fitted to the larger ships.

The Russian Navy
The role of the Russian Navy was to patrol and to protect, rather than to seek any strategic victory and, consequently, it had a relatively quiet war. In addition to the four main geographical Fleets—Baltic, Black Sea, Northern and Pacific—there were the Naval Air Force and Coastal Defence commands. The Baltic Fleet saw action against the Finns and consisted for the most part of light, shallow draught ships, supported by a couple of battleships and cruisers. The Black Sea Fleet centred on one battleship and six cruisers, whilst the Arctic and Pacific Fleets had no capital ships, but numerous destroyers and submarines. The Fleets were organised into flotillas in naval defence sectors and within these sectors, warships of a similar type were grouped into brigades. These brigades had several divisions varying widely in size from four to 20 ships, depending on their sizes.

The United States Navy
The American Navy always viewed the Pacific Ocean as the most important naval theatre of war and as a result concentrated most of its effort in that area. That said, the support given by the American Navy to the Royal Navy in the Battle of the Atlantic was an essential component of the eventual victory. In 1942 the US Atlantic Fleet was organised around no less than seven battleships, eight aircraft carriers and 12 cruisers.

Following the Japanese attack on the American Pacific Fleet in Pearl Harbor, the American Navy took a while to get into its stride. Fortunately, its three aircraft carriers were absent from Pearl Harbor at the time of the attack and these formed the basis of the new force. During 1942 the Americans began to regain the initiative and added a number of capital ships to their Pacific Fleet. The Carrier Fleet operated no less than 27 aircraft carriers of various sizes, some carrying as many as 90 aircraft each, whilst carriers with a capacity for 40 aircraft were fairly common. By April 1944, the United States 5th Fleet deployed in the Pacific a total of nineteen aircraft carriers, six battleships and six cruisers. The 5th Fleet was divided into a number of Task Forces, each of which was a self-contained formation usually consisting of three aircraft carriers supported by battleships and cruisers. It should not be forgotten either that the American submarine force carried out a vital and highly effective blockade against Japanese ports which strangled that country's economy.

HMS *Terpsichore*, a "T" Class destroyer, in January 1944.

The United States Marine Corps were continually engaged in the Pacific theatre, gaining a reputation for tenacity and sheer 'guts' for fighting a determined and often fanatical enemy during their 'island hopping' battles. In order to provide tactical air support to the Marines, the Corps had their own Air Corps of initially ten squadrons, expanded to over 130 by the end of hostilities.

The Ships
In order to provide some indication as to the size, performance and weaponry of the warships of the war, some representative types have been selected.

AUSTRALIA

Sydney
Type: Light cruiser   Speed: 32 knots
Main armament: 8×6"
Secondary armament: 8×4", 12×0.5", 8 tubes

FRANCE

Strasbourg
Type: Battleship   Speed: 31.5 knots
Tonnage: 26,500   Main armament: 8×13"
Secondary armament: 16×5.1", 8×37 mm, 32×13.2 mm

Richelieu
Type: Battleship   Speed: 32 knots
Tonnage: 35,000   Main armament: 8×15"
Secondary armament: 12×4", 60×40 mm, 50×20 mm

GERMANY

Admiral Graf Spree
Type: Pocket battleship   Speed: 27 knots
Tonnage: 12,100   Main armament: 6×11"
Secondary armament: 6×6", 8×5.9", 6×10.5 cm a/a, 8 tubes

Prinz Eugen
Type: Heavy cruiser   Speed: 32 knots
Tonnage: 16,230   Main armament: 8×8"
Secondary armament: 12×4.1", 12×37 mm, 28×20 mm

VIIA, VIIC
Type: Submarines   Speed: 8 knots
Tonnage: 857 (VIIIA), 871 (VIIC)
Main armament: 5×21" torpedo tubes
Secondary armament: 1×35", 2×20 mm guns

ITALY

Andrea Doria
Type: Battleship   Speed: 27 knots
Tonnage: 22,964   Main armament: 10×12.6"
Secondary armament: 12×5.2", 10×3.5", 19×37 mm

Vittorio Veneto
Type: Battleship   Speed: 30 knots
Tonnage: 35,000   Main armament: 9×15"
Secondary armament: 12×6", 4×4.7", 12×3.5", 20×37 mm,
32×20 mm

Bartolomeo Colleoni Class
Type: Light cruisers   Speed: 37 knots
Tonnage: 5,100 tons   Main armament: 4×6"
Secondary armament: 6×3.9", 3×21" tubes

JAPAN

Akagi
Type: Aircraft carrier   Speed: 31 knots
Tonnage: 36,500   Main armament: 2×8"
Secondary armament: 12×4.7", 28×25 mm
Aircraft: 90

Kongo
Type: Battleship   Speed: 30 knots
Tonnage: 31,720   Main armament: 8×14"
Secondary armament: 14×6", 8×5", 10×25 mm

Yamato

Type: Battleship   Speed: 27 knots
Tonnage: 64,170   Main armament: 9×18"
Secondary armament: 6×6.1", 12×5", 87×25 mm, 4×13 mm

Myoko

Type: Heavy cruiser   Speed: 33 knots
Tonnage: 13,380   Main armament: 10×8"
Secondary armament: 8×5", 8×25 mm, 4×13 mm

ROYAL NAVY

Glorious

Type: Aircraft carrier   Speed: 28 knots
Tonnage: 22,450   Main armament: 12×4"
Secondary armament: 32×2 pdr

Howe

Type: Battleship   Speed: 28 knots
Tonnage: 35,000   Main armament: 10×14"
Secondary armament: $16\times5\frac{1}{4}$", 48×2 pdr, 1×40 mm, 7×20 mm

Prince of Wales

Type: Battleship   Speed: 28 knots
Tonnage: 35,000   Main armament: 10×14"
Secondary armament: $16\times5\frac{1}{4}$", 48×2 pdr, 1×40 mm, 7×20 mm

Hood

Type: Battle cruiser   Speed: 31 knots
Tonnage: 42,100   Main armament: 8×15"
Secondary armament: 14×4", 24×2 pdr

Exeter

Type: Heavy cruiser   Speed: 32 knots
Tonnage: 8,400   Main armament: 6×8"
Secondary armament: 4×4", 2×2 pdr

Flower Class

Type: Corvette   Speed: 16 knots
Tonnage: 925   Main armament: 1×4"
Secondary armament: 2×2 pdr

RUSSIA

Oktyabrskaya Revolutsia
Type: Battleship   Speed: 23 knots
Tonnage: 23,606   Main armament: 12×12"
Secondary armament: 12×4.7", 8×3", 12×37 mm

Kirov
Type: Cruiser   Speed: 35 knots
Tonnage: 8,800   Main armament: 9×7.1"
Secondary armament: 8×4", 6×13 mm

UNITED STATES

Hornet
Type: Aircraft carrier   Speed: 33 knots
Tonnage: 20,000   Main armament: 8×5"
Secondary armament: 16×1.1", 23×30 mm
Aircraft: 80

Ameer
Type: Escort aircraft carrier   Speed: 18 knots
Tonnage: 11,300   Main armament: 2×4"
Secondary armament: 16×40 mm, 20×20 mm
Aircraft: 18–24

Alabama
Type: Battleship   Speed: 28 knots
Tonnage: 35,000   Main armament: 9×16"
Secondary armament: 20×5", 48×40 mm

In wargaming terms, it is comparatively rare for warships to be deployed simultaneously on the table top with land forces. Granted, there are some exceptions, amphibious landings spring to mind for example, but the nearest that the capital ships come to involvement is generally providing 'off table' gun fire support. The reasons for this are not too hard to find—a warship model built to the same scale as say a 1/72 tank would be truly enormous and would have to be deployed quite a distance away from the table. Usually, the warships used in naval wargaming are in either 1/1250 or 1/3000 scales, rendering a typical capital ship—say a battleship—about two inches long and at the most, half an inch high. As a result of this, such diminutive warships look downright silly on the same table as 1/72 or even 1/300 scale tanks and vehicles.

Interestingly enough, in their 1/600 scale white metal Coastal Forces series, Skytrex offer compatible vehicles—principally intended as landing craft 'loads'—but no infantry. The Japanese company Skywave also produce compatible scale aircraft, installations and vehicles in their 1/700 scale series of plastic kits. Thus, to a limited degree "sea and shore" can be depicted in the same wargame, but such a situation cannot really feature deep water warships.

In terms then of purely Fleet actions, an intriguing change came over naval warfare during the war. The concept of heavily-gunned battleships shooting at one another over huge distances (14" guns for example could engage targets at 16,000 yards) was replaced by that of aircraft supplying the hitting power. The Battle of North Cape in 1943, which saw the sinking of the German pocket battleship *Scharnhorst* by units of the Royal Navy, is often considered as being the last 'big gun' naval action. The 'new' type of warfare is perhaps typified by the Battle of the Coral Sea early in May 1942, where the opposing American and Japanese Fleets never actually saw one another, all the fighting being carried out by carrier-based naval aircraft.

The rules suggested below cater for engagements between warships at sea rather than any combined operations, and the scenarios reflect the ship-against-ship and aircraft-against-ship type of action. There is a school of thought amongst naval wargamers that, lacking a playing area of tennis court proportions, naval actions cannot meaningfully be played out. Such a view has a degree of credibility but, by scaling down ranges and so forth, naval battles *can* be fought on the wargames table, especially if the smaller-scale ship models are utilised.

THE RULES

Movement

When considering the speeds of the various warships, the wargamer once again has the problem of comparing the speed claimed by the manufacturers against economical cruising speeds. In point of fact, the wargamer can utilise both rates. Within the context of a campaign, cruising speeds and economy of fuel are of paramount importance—in the heat of battle, however, such considerations are secondary to self-preservation and full speed is frequently required. Since these rules are intended essentially as 'battle' rules, then we can for once consider the ship's maximum speed as being relevant. The ground (should that be sea?) scale adopted is 1 cm per knot of speed; thus a model ship whose historical predecessor steamed along at 25 knots would cover 25 cm (250 mm, roughly 10") on the wargames table. Eyebrows might be raised at the concept of ships operating continuously at full speed, but I stress that these are tactical rules which are only intended to apply for the duration of an engagement.

Firing

The main guns carried by battleships, battle-cruisers and cruisers were heavy and there is no avoiding this fact—indeed such heavy calibres were the very reason for the ships' existence. When considering firing, there are three aspects which need addressing: range, accuracy and effect.

Range

When dealing with naval gunnery ranges, a maximum of 20,000 yards is probably a sufficiently reasonable upper limit to set. As the war progressed, radar became increasingly sophisticated, as did range-finding equipment, so wargamers wishing to exceed this figure have some historical right on their side, but 20,000 yards will be sufficient for our present purposes. Initially the 1 mm = 1 yard was considered, but 20,000 mm equates to approximately 66 feet which is clearly unworkable. Instead the range band system, similar to that employed for our land-based artillery, is employed. Basically, one foot on the table is reckoned as being 2,500 yards so that the shells from a ship firing at a 'range' of 3,800 yards would fall between two and three feet away. If required, the units of a foot could be further sub-divided into inches or whatever, thus reducing the range band into smaller distances. This may be seen as an unnecessary refinement, but I offer it as a suggestion. To establish that the range has been correctly found, two ordinary dice are rolled and their totalled score compared to the table below:-

Range to target	Dice score needed for hit
0–2,500	Automatic hit
2,501–5,000	2
5,001–7,500	3
7,501–10,000	4,5
10,001–12,500	6,7
12,501–15,000	8,9
15,001–17,500	10,11
17,501–20,000	12

When a ship is firing its guns on subsequent moves *at the same target*, then the ranging dice needed to achieve the correct range is reduced by one each time. Thus, a ship firing at 16,000 yards needs a 10 or 11 initially, and if this is not achieved, then on the next move a 9, 10 or 11 will suffice. If contact is still not made, then on the next move a score of 8 or above will register a potential hit. The idea behind this mechanism is that, given the existence of radar and/or range-finding equipment to correct the aim, a ship's guns will eventually find the range to straddle its target. It must be stressed that this only applies to ships continuously firing at the same target, even if they are both moving—if another is selected, then the ranging-in process starts anew.

Accuracy
Having established the range, the accuracy of the shell also needs to be considered. Here there are two factors: the distance between the two vessels and the size of the target. Based on the premise that the further a shell has to travel, then the less chance there is of a hit, we can utilise further the above table to provide probable results at varying ranges. Thus, once the range of say 12,000 yards has been found with a 6 or a 7, a further 6 or 7 is now needed to certify a hit on that target. If however, the target is a battleship, it would be a good deal easier to hit at 12,000 yards than, say, a corvette. To reflect this, the ship types have been divided into four classes as follows:-

Class One: Aircraft carriers and battleships
Class Two: Battle cruisers and heavy cruisers
Class Three: Light cruisers
Class Four: Destroyers, frigates and corvettes

If a ship is firing at a target ship which is in the same class as itself or any of those below it, then the firer has the customary one attempt per move to hit it. If however, the target is in a class *above* that of the firer, then the ship carrying out the firing may have two attempts at scoring an accurate hit in the same move. Thus, a battleship firing at a destroyer has only one attempt per move, while the destroyer firing back has two.

Effect

The number of guns firing and the weight of their shells are the two points for deliberation here. Wargamers can consider the firing mechanisms outlined above as applying to the whole ship, a turret (which can contain a varying number of guns) or the individual guns themselves. Whichever method is selected, the mechanics of firing in themselves are not affected. Once it achieves a hit, a shell from, say, a 14" gun is going to cause damage to its target—the amount varying of course, dependent on the size of that target. This is decided by allocating a 'damage value' to a specific shell or rather group of shells:-

Calibre of shells	Damage points caused on contact
18"–14"	10
13"–10"	8
9"–7"	6
5"–4"	4
Below 4"	2

Thus a 4.7" shell, landing on target, will cause 4 points worth of damage to its unfortunate recipient. That said, we need to establish how much damage a particular ship can withstand. For this, the four classes of warship listed earlier are used. In this example 'ship firing' is used for the sake of simplicity, but the wargamer can formulate adaptations of the system for gun or turret firings. Class One ships can absorb 100 points worth of damage, Class Two 80, Class Three 60 and Class Four 40. So, a Class Two ship, say a battle cruiser, can take eight direct hits from 14" to 18" guns, whilst a Class Four frigate can survive only two such hits. Likewise, a Class One battleship is unlikely to be too worried, initially at least, at the prospect of being battered by the 8" guns of a cruiser. The damage caused to the target ship by the shells would probably be cumulative, with the performance of that ship being rendered increasingly less effective. To cover this, the following table has been constructed:-

Damage points remaining				
Class 1	Class 2	Class 3	Class 4	Effect of damage
100	80	60	40	None
75	60	45	35	Speed reduced by half
50	40	30	20	Gunnery reduced by half
25	20	15	10	Speed and gunnery reduced to a quarter of the original

Once the total of damage points remaining falls to nought, the ship in question is considered sunk. It is readily appreciated that all this is quite arbitrary—the first salvo could cripple the target's steering gear and, if the target is an aircraft carrier, is its ability to fly off planes affected? These are valid points and the damage points table can be made as simple or complex as the wargamer wishes. The preceding table, although eminently usable as it stands, is intended ony as a guide. On the reduction of gunnery capability due to damage sustained—if turret or gun firing is being used, reduce this in proportion to the damage suffered. If the ship firing is used, then the ship fires every other turn; when gunnery has been reduced to half, every second turn when down to a quarter.

Torpedoes and submarines

Torpedoes may be fired by any ship apart from an aircraft carrier. Class 1 and 2 ships carry three, Classes 3 and 4 have eight each. With regard to effect, the torpedo is classed as a 12" gun, as it is for accuracy. The reduced range of a torpedo is reflected by considering it to have a maximum range of 10,000 yards. A submarine can also carry eight torpedoes, again firing in the usual manner. Due to the inescapable fact that submarines operated under the water, they are difficult to incorporate into a wargame. The sheer effectiveness of a submarine lies in its ability to 'sneak up' on its intended victim, but it does have to float up to periscope depth in order to fire its torpedoes. Such a target is considered as being impossible to hit with gun fire and depth-charges are used instead. As their name suggests, these devices are explosive charges which, after being fired from surface vessels, drop into the sea to explode at a predetermined, but variable, depth. For the purposes of these rules, the submarine is considered to be a Class Two ship, and the depth charge a 4"–5" shell. Depth charges may only be dropped by Class One vessels, who each carry six. Now, a submarine under water is pretty difficult to hit and the rules are amended as follows.

There is no automatic hit against a submarine and the maximum 'range' for a depth charge is 5,000 yards. This is divided into two bands—0 to 2,500 yards where a 3 or 4 on one dice is needed, and

2,501 to 5,000 yards with a 5 or 6 needed for ranging. Accuracy is particularly difficult when chasing a submarine and only a double 3 or 4, 5 or 6 (dependent on range) scored on two dice will achieve a hit. In terms of damage, a submarine is classified as a Class Three ship, i.e. able to take 80 points worth of damage before sinking.

Naval Aircraft

The main function of the carrier-based naval strike aircraft is as a bomber and it is in this role that we shall use such aircraft in our wargames. The torpedo bomber fulfilled a somewhat more minor role, but we will also look at this type of air attack. The rules for aircraft, particularly those covering ground attack which are outlined in Chapter 10, can be utilised but, to conserve space, these will not be repeated in full again here.

The main problem is for the attacking plane (which is regarded as carrying two bombs) to actually hit its intended target, so the bomb is once again regarded as being fired by a mortar. Once a hit is achieved, the bomb is counted as being a 6" shell, causing six points worth of damage. Torpedoes delivered by aircraft (one per model) are treated in exactly the same manner as those launched by ship or submarine. The only difference is that to release the torpedo the aircraft in question must be under 100 mm, otherwise the torpedo is considered lost.

Any defensive anti-aircraft fire put up by ships can be dealt with using the appropriate rules from the air warfare chapter.

SCENARIOS

Giving the Italians a bit of Pasta-ing . . .

It is early November 1940 and the Italian battleships *Andrea Doria, Conte di Cavour, Caio Duilo* and *Littorio* lie at anchor at their main base of Taranto in south east Italy. An attack, the first of its type in history, is mounted by a number of Fairey Swordfish torpedo bombers launched from the decks of the Royal Naval aircraft carrier, HMS *Illustrious*. Some 21 aircraft fly in to carry out the raid, which in actual fact sunk the *Cavour*, beached the *Duilo* and damaged the *Littorio*. It is worth recording that the after effects of the action went further than the straightforward damage to three capital ships of the Italian Navy. British naval power in that crucial theatre of war, the Mediterranean, was re-established and, in terms of morale, the Italians did not recover from the Taranto raid.

This scenario seeks to recreate this attack and examine the wargames potential of the torpedo-carrying aircraft against the defensive firepower of a surface vessel. While 1/72 and lesser-scale models or kits of the Fairey Swordfish ('The Stringbag' as it was

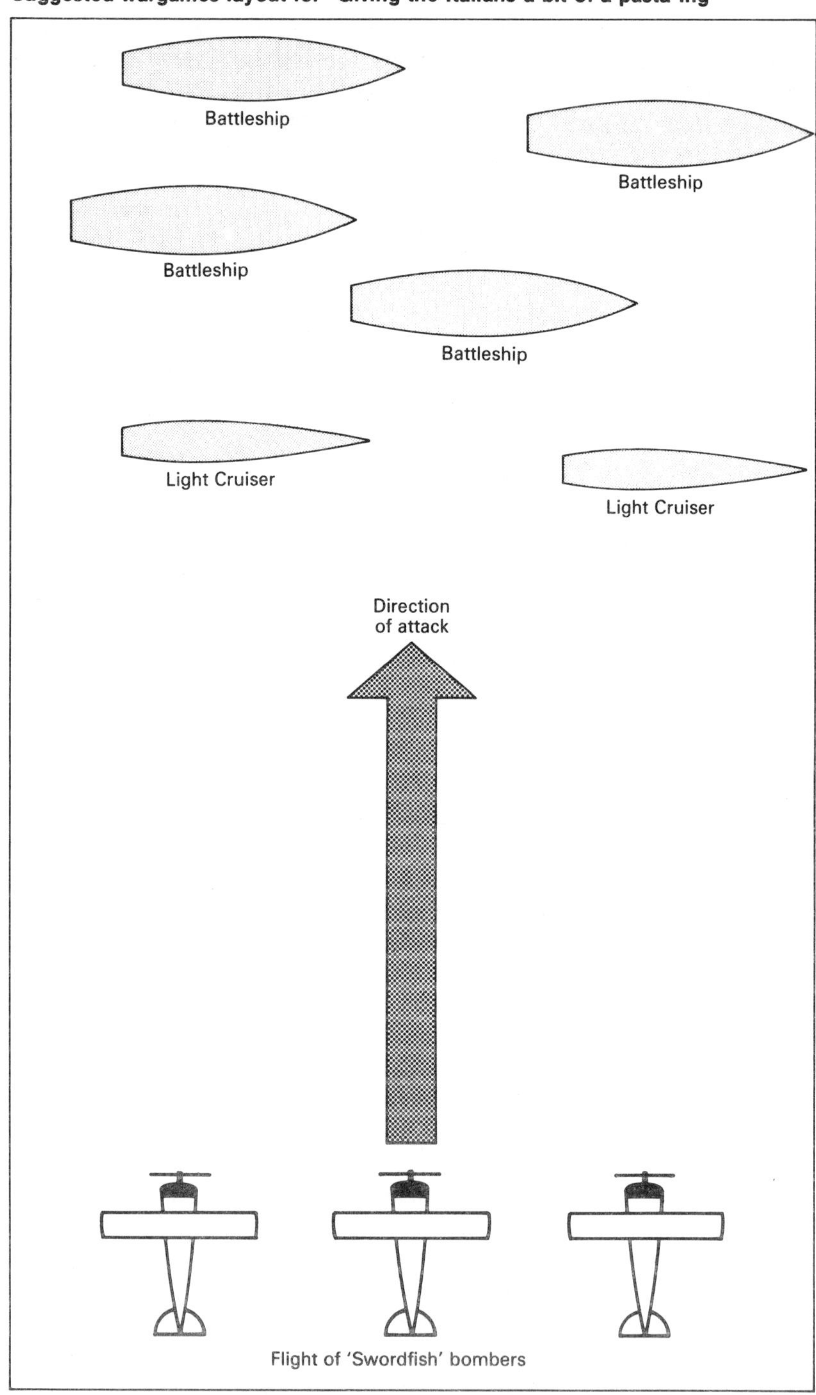
Battleship
Battleship
Battleship
Battleship
Light Cruiser
Light Cruiser
Direction
of attack
Flight of 'Swordfish' bombers

affectionately termed at the time) do exist, they are relatively rare. I suggest that really any model planes can be used for this particular scenario but, should the purist wish to stick out in favour of using the actual Swordfish, this is a commendable attitude. Although the intention is to fight the action out on a one-to-one basis, not all of the 21 aircraft who took part need to be purchased, for the attack was delivered in waves, meaning that the same models can be used over again, which is good news if the wargamer is assembling plastic kits! In the trial runs for this scenario, six model planes were found to be about the right number. There were only three Italian battleships damaged, but these were anchored amongst smaller warships and the wargamer may wish to offer at least a token representation of this. In its most basic form, the scenario only calls for the presence of the four 'heavies', but any additional dressing adds to the appearance of the wargame.

Sufficient information has been given in the rules for this battle to be fought out using them. In lieu of more detailed information, the three battleships can be given the same armament as that of the *Andrea Doria* and the support ships that of the *Bartolomeo Colleoni* Class light cruiser, both of which are quoted earlier in the text. There is no need to represent HMS *Illustrious* or indeed any other Royal Naval warship, for it was purely the aircraft which did the damage. Will the planes in the scenario be as successful as their historical counterparts? Only the wargamer can decide.

Ill Met by Moonlight...

In October 1942, the Americans decided to reinforce Guadalcanal and to land more troops on the island. Accordingly, a convoy was organised with an escort of warships. As the troops were being put ashore, these warships drew off to provide a blocking force against any Japanese interference, since it was known that units of the Japanese navy were operating to the south of Guadalcanal. What was not known, however, was just how near the enemy was. The Japanese had also decided to put men on the island and, as the troop carrying ships neared the coastline, their escorts drew off and began to close in to provide gunnery support. Neither side were aware of the other's presence and, as the American warships steamed north-westwards, they stumbled across their Japanese counterparts sailing south-east. During the night of 11th–12th October 1942, the resultant battle of Cape Esperance took place.

The American ships under an Admiral Scott consisted of the heavy cruisers *San Francisco* (the flag ship) and *Salt Lake City*, the light cruisers *Boise* and *Helena* and finally the destroyers *Buchanan, Duncan, Farenholt, Laffy* and *McCalla*. The Japanese force led by Admiral Goto consisted of the heavy cruisers *Aoba,*

Suggested wargame layout for "Ill met by moonlight"

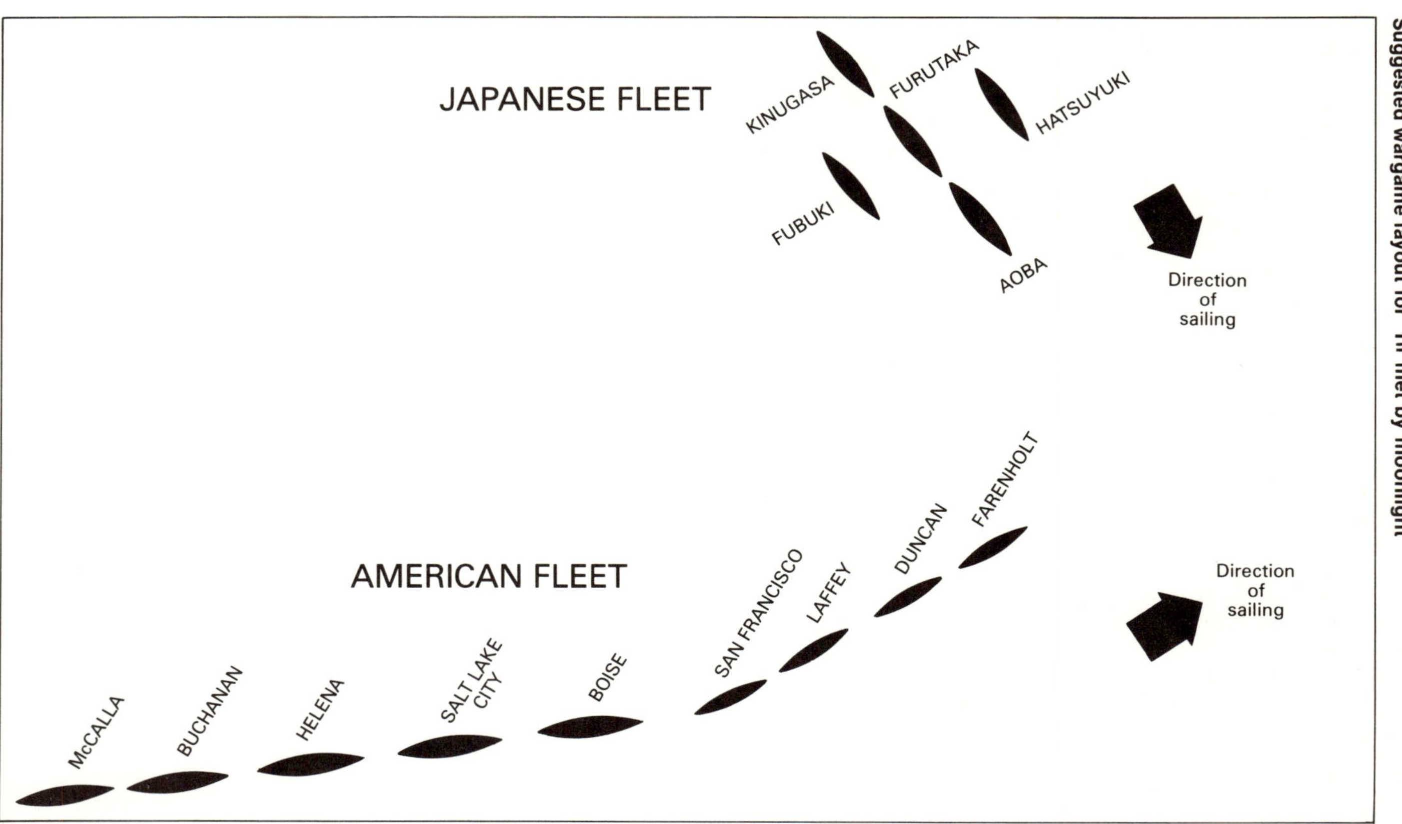

Kinugasa and *Furutaka* and two destroyers, *Fubuki* and *Hatsuyuki*. The following table of generalised information may be found to be of use when recreating this scenario:-

Ship	Tonnage	Speed	Main Guns	Secondary Armament
US H Cruiser	12,000	32k	9×8"	8×5" 32×40 27×20 mm
US L Cruiser	6,607	31k	10×5.9"	8×40 mm
US Destroyer	2,050	36k	5×5"	10×40, 20×20 mm
JP H Cruiser	13,380	34k	10×8"	8×5" 8×25 4×13 mm
JP Destroyer	2,090	34k	4×5"	14×25 mm 9×24" tubes

Historically, the Americans had a destroyer sunk and a light cruiser badly damaged, while the Japanese suffered the loss of a heavy cruiser and a destroyer, with another two destroyers being damaged. It will be an interesting exercise to re-enact the battle, fought at night it will be remembered, and see if the historical outcome is either matched or reversed.

Kits and Models

Airfix

A small range of 1/600 scale full hull plastic model kits, an even shorter range of relatively 1/1200 and an RAF Rescue Launch in 1/72 scale, again full hull.

Davco

One of the Skytrex group, this company produces some well-detailed 1/3000 white metal merchantmen and warships. (Model Figures & Hobbies).

Matchbox

A range of white metal 1/1200 scale waterline models.

ESCI

This company has a small range of 1/1200 waterline plastic kits featuring American, British, Italian, German and Japanese warships.

Fujimi

An interesting range of 1/700 plastic kit models, including aircraft.

Italeri

A smallish range of plastic kits in 1/720 scale.

Ensign

Lindbergh

A small range of plastic kits of varying scales.

Matchbox

A reasonable range of 1/7000 scale waterline plastic kits and one 1/72 kit of a Flower Class corvette.

Revell
Offer limited ranges of plastic kits in 1/350, 1/570 and 1/720 scales.

Skywave
A very useful range of 1/700 plastic kits, which includes installations, e.g. submarine pens and such interesting items as landing craft.

Tamiya
A sometimes difficult to obtain 1/700 range of plastic kits.

Triton
Another Skytrex company who manufacture some interesting 1/600 scale Coastal Forces items under the heading "The Fight for the Narrow Seas". Cast in white metal, the range covers motor torpedo boats, E boats, PT boats and light escort vessels.

Rules
General Quarters by L. Brom, Part 1: World War II & Campaigns
War At Sea MOD Games
World War II Naval Wargames, by R. Ellard & J. Hammond, Skytrex
All the above rule sets are available from Quartermaster's Stores, 17–19, West Wycombe Road, High Wycombe, Bucks HP11 2LQ.

Books
Carter B. *Naval Wargames: World War I & World War II* David & Charles 1975
Dunn P. *Sea Battle Games* MAP 1970
Featherstone D. *Naval Wargames* Stanley Paul 1965
Kennedy L. *Menace: The Life and Death of the Tirpitz* Sidgwick & Jackson 1979
Kennedy L. *Pursuit: The Sinking of the Bismarck* Collins 1974
Lund P. & Ludlam H. *The War of the Landing Craft* W. Foulsham & Co 1976
Mallman Showell J. *U-Boats Under the Swastika* Ian Allen 1973
Middlebrook M. & Mahoney P. *Battleship* Allen Lane 1977
Muggenthaler A. *German Raiders of World War II* Robert Hale 1978
Smith P. *Arctic Victory* William Kimber 1975
Waldron T. & Gleeson J. *The Frogmen* Elmfield Press 1950

Section III—The War in the Air

We now turn our attention to the war in the air and begin by looking at how the combatant countries organised their respective air forces.

The German Air Force

The German Air Force, or Luftwaffe, was created in early 1935, with Hermann Goering appointed Air Minister. With a strength of some 1,000 aircraft and 20,000 personnel, the Luftwaffe saw active service in the Spanish Civil War 1937–39 and as a result gained useful combat experience. In March 1938, the Luftwaffe transported men and equipment during the annexation of Austria, an exercise which, it is interesting to record, saw the Austrian Air Force incorporated into the Luftwaffe. It is true to say that by the outbreak of the war, the German Air Force was a highly-trained and well-equipped element of the German armed forces. The early campaigns in Poland, Norway, Denmark and France proved both the value of the Luftwaffe and its capability to support ground operations.

Reporting to the Luftwaffe High Command were four Air Fleets with headquarters in Berlin, Brunswick, Munich and Vienna. These fleets were divided into flying corps which in turn were composed of flying units, the nature and number of which were dependent on the role of the unit. Within the corps were the Geschwader which could perhaps be roughly equated to a brigade formation. There were three of these, each covering a different type of aircraft—bombers, dive bombers and fighters. Each Geschwader consisted of three or four groups, each of three to four squadrons and the squadrons themselves each had between 10 and 12 aircraft.

The organisation of the Luftwaffe's ground forces was a little complex, in that the parachute units were, uniquely, a part of the Air Force, whilst air landing troops—infantrymen trained in the role of airborne landings—remaining as part of the army, were not.

The Finnish Air Force

The Finnish Air Force was part of the Finnish army and was organised into three Flying Regiments. The 1st dealt with dive bombing, ground attack and reconnaissance and mustered four squadrons each of 12 aircraft. The 2nd operated fighter defence and had two squadrons each of 24 aircraft, whilst the 3rd handled bombing and long range reconnaissance with two eight plane squadrons.

The French Air Force

The French Air Force came into being in April 1933 and was divided into five regions, Aix-en-Provence, Dijon, North Africa, Paris and Tours. Each of these regions was further sub-divided into two districts but the largest flying formations were air divisions. These each had two or three brigades and each brigade was of two or three squadrons. As war broke out, the French could call on 1,200 fighters, 1,300 bombers and perhaps 800 reconnaissance aircraft all of which were outdated and inferior to those of the Luftwaffe.

Most of the inland, as opposed to the coastal, anti-aircraft artillery came under the jurisdiction of the Air Ministry and was organised into five battalions, each of three 75 mm batteries and a searchlight battalion.

Some Free French pilots took part in the Battle of Britain, whilst the first Free French RAF squadron was No 340 'Isle de France'. The 1st Company, Free French Parachute Troops was also formed and transferred to army control. One Free French squadron operated with the RAF in the Western Desert and there were also units fighting in Eritrea, the Middle East, Syria and the Mediterranean.

The organisation of the Vichy Air Force was of six fighter groups, two night fighter squadrons, six bomber groups, two ground-attack groups and three reconnaissance groups. A group was usually of two squadrons, each having 12 aircraft. Once the Germans occupied Vichy France these formations were disbanded and the aircraft impounded.

The Italian Royal Air Force

It was 1923 when the Italian Royal Air Force came into being and after a promising start, was on the decline by the time war broke out. As a result, whilst the Italian pilots fought well enough, the Air Force did not achieve very much during the war. The largest formation was the air fleet which consisted of two or more fighter or bomber divisions. Each division had two air brigades, each of two or three wings. The wing was formed by two or three squadrons, which each fielded nine aircraft—six in bomber units—with three in reserve. In Libya the Italians had four bomber wings and one of fighters. There were also three groups of fighters and just over two of reconnaissance aircraft. In North Africa by 1942 were 12 fighter groups, one of dive bombers and three of bombers.

The Japanese Air Force

The Japanese army and navy each operated their own air force. The army service provided ground support and air cover and was organised into five air armies. The division, which consisted of two brigades, was the largest formation. The brigades had three or four regiments which were divided into a like number of companies, which, consisting of nine planes, were the operational units. The naval section was organised as the Combined Air Fleet which consisted of the carrier based 1st Air Fleet and the shore based 11th Air Fleet. These fleets were made up of flotillas, which in turn had two or more groups of between 12 and 36 aircraft. The usual fighting element was the division, which, like the army company, consisted of nine aircraft.

The Polish Air Force

The Polish Air Force was virtually destroyed in the opening days of the German Polish Campaign in September 1939. The greater part of the Air Force was allocated to the ground forces along the Polish-German border, but some units formed a central reserve which was called the Dispositional Air Force. This formation mustered five fighter squadrons, eight bombing/reconnaissance squadrons, one for observation and four liaison units. A number of Polish pilots flew with the RAF and there were two Polish squadrons, Nos 302 and 303.

The Royal Air Force

As the war opened, the British Expeditionary Force was supported by two bomber/reconnaissance squadrons, four of fighters and six army co-operation squadrons. Further, there was what was termed an 'Advanced Air Striking Force' based in France and consisting of medium bombers. These two commands were united in 1940 and with the fall of France, all operational aircraft were moved back to the British Isles. To co-ordinate the defence of the United Kingdom during the Battle of Britain, the country was divided into four large

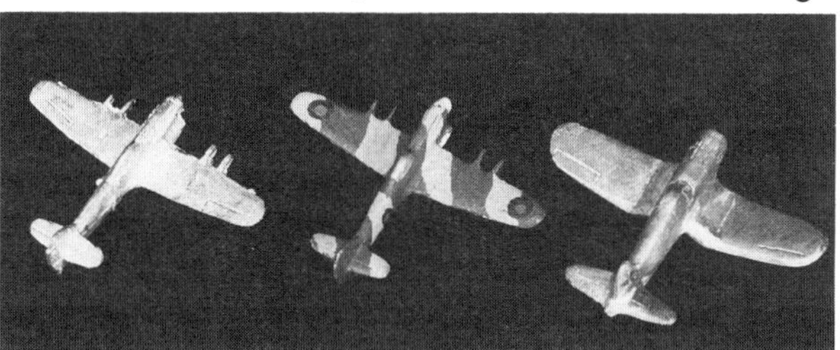

Some examples of the white metal small scale aircraft which are available —these are Allied aircraft.

The might of the Luftwaffe in small scale.

areas, each of which was allotted a fighter Group. The next formation was the sector which would control between two and five squadrons.

In the other theatres of war the RAF was short of aircraft. In addition to operations against the Italian Air Force, the opening of the campaign in Greece stretched the resources of Middle East Command even further, whilst in North Africa there were only four squadrons to cover the whole of Cyrenaica. By 1941 squadrons piloted by Commonwealth and allied crews swelled the numbers and by the end of the year there were over 27 squadrons deployed in the Western Desert. Far East Command operated three Groups in Ceylon, Burma and Singapore in co-operation with the Royal Indian Air Force. Operating from bases in India were eventually six Groups and once South East Asia Command was formed in 1944 there were over 60 RAF squadrons deployed. The air war over Europe saw the development of the specialist ground attack aircraft, which achieved considerable success against specialised and vital targets. The RAF was also active in Europe, carrying out bombing raids and providing support for the ground forces. By mid 1941 there were 45 squadrons of bombers and 50 two years later with perhaps only half that number being operational, but they did have the latest in aircraft. Many of the major bombing raids were carried out by four engined heavy bombers—at night so that the need for a fighter escort was reduced. Bomber Command was organised into seven Groups, each having several 'bases', each with six squadrons, of which there were 95 by the end of the war. Coastal Command, which operated escort, reconnaissance and strike squadrons consisted of four Groups which from early 1941 were under the control of the Admiralty. Despite an overall lack of aircraft, especially long range types, Coastal Command achieved successes against German submarines

The Fleet Air Arm was the air wing of the Royal Navy proper, which operated from capital ships and aircraft carriers.

The RAF Regiment was formed for airfield defence early in 1942 with the field squadron as its basic tactical unit. There were 185 men in a squadron which was composed of three rifle 'flights' as well as anti-aircraft, armoured car and support 'flights'.

The Soviet Air Force

The Russian Air Force also saw active service in the Spanish Civil War as well as during the war with Finland. The air force consisted of two sections, the Air Force of the Red Army and Long Range Bomber Force. The former operated in the ground attack and fighter capacity under the direct control of a military district, whilst the latter deployed tactically under the State Defence Commissar. Following a reorganisation after the war with Finland, the largest formation was the division of four to six regiments each of approximately 60 planes. The division usually contained a variety of aircraft types, as sometimes could the regiment. There were three types of regiment, which was the basic tactical formation—those of bombers, which had four squadrons each of 12 aircraft, nine of which were operational, fighters which fielded four squadrons of 15 and ground attack which was organised on the same lines as the fighter regiment. By 1941, the Russian Air Force was the largest in the world, but was in something of a mess due partly to the fact that it was under politically suitable, rather than capable leadership. Whilst initially overwhelmed by the Luftwaffe, Soviet air power began to gain in strength due to increased home production and the Allied Lend-Lease programme. These factors brought about another re-organisation which took place in late 1941 and yet another—this time largely to increase the size of combat units—in 1942. Ground attack regiments for example had a third squadron allocated, which meant that they then had 32 aircraft, rising to 40 a year later. By this time the regiment had four reserve aircraft and was sub-divided into three squadrons, each of 12 planes.

The United States

In June 1941 the United States of America Army Air Force came into being with a programme of rapid expansion, the pace of which increased following the Japanese attack on Pearl Harbor later that year. Originally eight air forces came into being, but between 1943–44 the Army Air Force doubled in size. The USAAF presence in the Mediterranean consisted of the 12th and 15th Air Forces, the former operating chiefly in North Africa, the latter (formed from the 12th) in Italy and Europe generally. The 5th operated in the Pacific, the 9th in the Middle East, whilst the 8th flew from British bases, carrying out hundreds of daytime bombing missions against German targets. Organisation of the USAAF tended to vary from theatre to theatre, but generally the smallest administrative unit was the group of two to four squadrons. The wing consisted of two groups and two wings of the same type of function formed a command. The air force would then consist of two or three of these commands, but it must be stressed that these command structures were very flexible.

The Aircraft

Having gained an idea of how the various countries organised their respective air forces, we now need to look at the aircraft which were in service during the war. To catalogue and analyse all the different types, along with the various production stages, would fill a book several times the size of this one. Instead, a selection of the main types is offered with some basic data which wargamers will find of interest. A popular production mark of each aircraft has been chosen as being representative of that particular genre of aeroplane.

Germany

Focke-Wulf Fw190G

In the mid-war period, the Fw190 became the Luftwaffe's most important tactical attack weapon.
Maximum speed: 419 mph   Range: 497 miles
Bomb load: 165 lbs   Weaponry: Four mgs

Heinkel He 111H-22

Receiving a thorough workout in the Spanish Civil War, the twin-engined Heinkel bomber was progressively modified as the war continued. By the end of the war it was still in service, but hopelessly out of date. By this time most Heinkels were relegated to transport duties, but a few were refitted to air launch the V-1 rocket.
Maximum speed: 258 mph   Range: 1,212 miles
Bomb load: Typically 4,410 lbs   Weaponry: Seven mgs

Junkers Ju 87B-2

The famous Stuka dive bomber, the Ju 87B was widely used as a 'terror weapon' in the early days of the war and enjoyed an unrivalled reputation. As the Allies gained in both experience and numbers, the Stukas proved to be remarkably easy to 'kill' and were withdrawn from the dive bombing role.
Maximum speed: 238 mph   Range: 620 miles
Bomb load: 1,102 lbs   Weaponry: Two to four mgs

Messerschmitt Bf109E

Although apparently difficult to fly, the various marks of the Bf109 fighter were produced in huge numbers. Once again, the aeroplane was tested in the Spanish Civil War and was the Luftwaffe's main fighter.

Maximum speed: 350 mph   Range: 435 miles
Bomb load: 551 lbs   Weaponry: Four or five mgs

Messerschmitt Bf110G-4d

An efficient long range bomber escort machine, the Bf110 had a good start to the war in terms of performance, but later was no match for Allied fighters. Operating against the RAF night time bombing raids, the aircraft also did sterling service as a night fighter.
Maximum speed: 342 mph   Range: 560 miles
Bomb load: up to 2,205 lbs on earlier marks
Weaponry: Six mgs, two 210 mm rocket tubes, 37 mm cannon

Italy

Savoia-Marchetti S.M.79-II Sparviero

This three-engined bomber was another aircraft which saw service in Spain, where it performed well. One of its main roles was as a torpedo bomber in the Mediterranean theatre, where it also provided good service.
Maximum speed: 267 mph   Range: 1,242 miles
Bomb load: 2,645 lbs or two torpedoes
Weaponry: Four or five mgs

Japan

Aichi D3A1 Val

A carrier based dive bomber, the D3A1 took part in the attack on the American fleet in Pearl Harbor.
Maximum speed: 242 mph   Range: 915 miles
Bomb load: 187 lbs   Weaponry: Three mgs

Mitsubishi A6M2-N Zero

The main Japanese fighter of the war, the Zero operated from aircraft carriers and shore bases.
Maximum speed: 271 mph   Range: 1,107 miles
Bomb load: 132 lbs   Weaponry: Four machine guns

Royal Air Force

Avro Lancaster

Selected here as being typical of the RAF's heavy bombers, the Lancaster carried out countless bombing missions against targets in Europe.
Maximum speed: 287 mph
Range: 1,660 to 2,530 miles, dependent on bomb load
Bomb load: 14,000 lbs   Weaponry: Up to nine mgs

De Havilland D.H.98 Mosquito MkIII
A most versatile aircraft which operated in photo-reconnaissance, fighter, night fighter and fighter bomber roles, the sheer speed of the 'Mossie' was perhaps it's greatest asset.
Maximum speed: 380 mph   Range: 1,860 miles
Bomb load: 2,000 lbs
Weaponry: Four 20 mm cannon, four mgs

Hawker Hurricane Mk II
One of the RAF's two main fighters and often for no real reason overshadowed by the Spitfire, the Hurricane was a rugged, reliable aircraft which was often used in differing roles.
Maximum speed: 322 mph   Range: 505 miles
Bomb load: 500 lbs
Weaponry: Eight mgs or four 20 mm cannon or two 40 mm cannon

Supermarine Spitfire Mk V
The most numerous fighter of the RAF during the war, the production of the Spitfire went to several marks, XIX being the last.
Maximum speed: 374 mph   Range: 1,000 miles
Weaponry: Eight mgs., but a mix of 20 mm and 7.7 mm were often carried.

The Soviet Union

Lavochkin LaGG-3
Producing a good all round performance and possessing excellent manoeuvrability, the Lavochkin was an important Russian fighter.
Maximum speed: 348 mph   Range: 404 miles
Bomb load: 165 lbs (typically)
Weaponry: One 20 mm cannon, two mgs and six rockets

Yakovlev Yak-1
With a great performance on par with the LaGG-3, the Yak was produced in greater numbers than any other fighter of the war.
Maximum speed: 373 mph   Range: 520 miles
Bomb load: 110 or 220 lbs
Weaponry: One 20 mm cannon, two mgs and six rockets

United States

Boeing B-17C Flying Fortress
Surely the most famous American bomber, the B-17 carried out countless daytime bombing raids against enemy targets.
Maximum speed: 323 mph   Range: 1,100 miles

Bomb load: 6,000 lbs
Weaponry: Seven, later up to 13 mgs

Lockheed P38F Lightning
This twin-engined long range fighter was one of the best of its type.
Maximum speed: 395 mph   Range: 900 miles
Bomb load: 1,000 lbs
Weaponry: One 20 mm cannon, four mgs

North American B-25A Mitchell
This twin-engined medium bomber was supplied to virtually every Allied air force.
Maximum speed: 317 mph   Range: 2,000 miles
Bomb load: 2,000 lbs
Weaponry: Five mgs

North American P-51C Mustang
The manoeuvrable Mustang fighter proved to be more than a match for its German counterparts and was flown by many of the Allied air forces.
Maximum speed: 388 mph   Range: 750 miles
Bomb load: 1,000 lbs
Weaponry: Four or six mgs

9   Rules and Scenarios

Before moving into any detailed rules for the use of model aircraft in a wargame, there is an important question to consider. The main and unavoidable problem with air wargaming is that of the third dimension, the air. Infantry, vehicles and ships will all stand quite happily on the normal horizontal wargame playing surface and perform their respective functions. Model aircraft will not, and they need some sort of support mechanism before they can be used in a game. This problem is immediately apparent when one is considering air-to-air as opposed to air-to-ground combat. A number of years ago, a book on conducting air wargames appeared (*Air Battles in Miniature*, M. Spick, PSL 1978) in which the author suggested halving the model aircraft along their length and using the two halves to represent a side view of the aircraft. This meant that the wargame could be played out on a flat surface, be it flat or on a wall, with the models being attached with Blu-Tac or whatever. This fairly novel idea does not seem to have caught on and certainly I have never seen such a game being played. The method does however have its merits, which is why I have mentioned it.

So how can we move our model aircraft up into the wide blue yonder? Essentially there are four methods which will be discussed briefly here.

Hand-held

Obvious?—certainly, but undoubtedly the easiest and most flexible method open to the wargamer. Much will depend on the size of the model aircraft in question, in that the larger the scale, the easier the planes are to handle. To 'fly' a 1/72nd scale model which will project from the hand is a great deal easier than one in 1/200th scale which is about one third its size and tricky to hold. By holding the model, the wargamer can, albeit somewhat self-consciously, control the height and speed of the aircraft. Air-to-air combats as well as air-to-ground attacks are perfectly feasible by this method, but, dare it be said, each wargamer in lieu of additional appendages is restricted to using a maximum of two aircraft simultaneously.

Suspended

The models can be suspended from the ceiling on lengths of cotton, but this method tends to be fairly static, due to the necessary agility needed by the wargamer to shift continually the position of the aircraft. For two or three moves in a wargame, such a system is fine (and looks very presentable), but the sheer physical effort involved means that it quickly palls. There is the problem of reaching the ceiling, which from the edges of the table, is not too difficult but, once over the centre of the table, verges on the impossible. Models suffering from faulty suspension can also plummet downwards with a positively sickening crash, especially if they are of the plastic kit variety.

On posts

Using this method, a piece of dowelling of suitable length and diameter is fixed into a base, which then stands on the wargames table. A much smaller piece of dowel is then fixed into the side or on to the wing tip of the model aircraft. There are two methods of connecting the dowelling rod from the aircraft to the vertical length. Firstly, the dowelling from the plane can end in a plastic collar which can, in fact, be a short piece of plastic conduit, which is of a size just to fit with some friction over the main dowel, with a degree of friction sufficient to hold the aircraft in place. Alternatively, the main dowel rod can have a series of holes drilled in it along its length (height?) to accommodate the smaller rod extending from the model aircraft. Thus the height of the aircraft can be adjusted by moving the smaller dowelling rod up and down by whatever method it is fixed to the main post or rod. The position of the aircraft can be varied either by a circular movement using the main dowelling rod as an axis, or by simply moving the entire contraption, model and all.

On stands

Here again there are two methods, referred to as 'light' and 'heavy'. For the former, some fairly thin but rigid wire is used. This is built into a tripod, with one leg being much longer than the other two. How the three lengths of wire are fixed together is up to the individual wargamer, but it is worth pointing out that, whichever method is adopted, it needs to be fairly strong—soldering, or the use of epoxy resin glue is recommended. The three similarly-sized short legs of the tripod form a base or stand for the model on the table, whilst the 'long' end fits into a small hole drilled into the underside of the model aircraft. If several stands are made in this manner and the length of the longer arm varied, then the aircraft can operate at varying heights by the simple expedient of the wargamer changing its stand. Also, of course, the entire stand can be moved in keeping

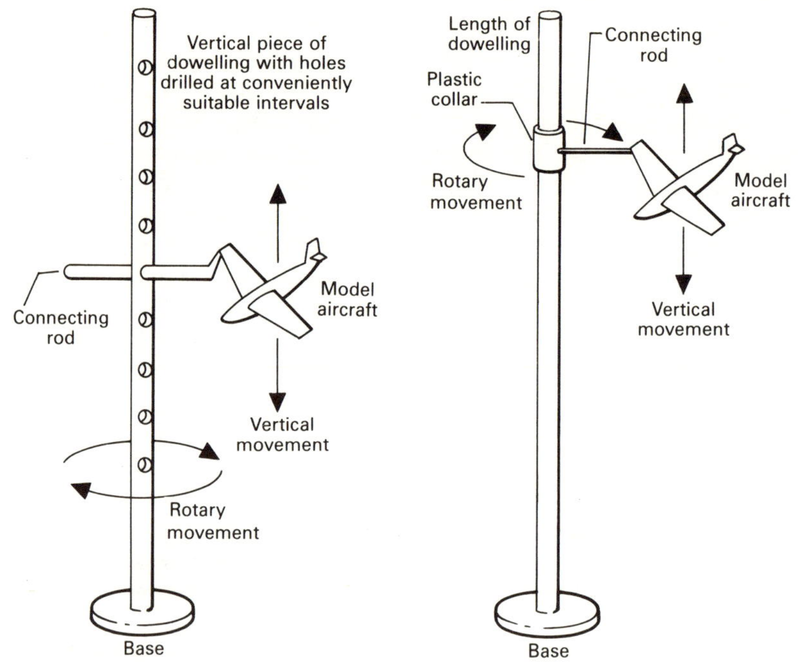

Methods of holding model aircraft.

with the aircraft's progress, but the circular motion facilitated by the previous method is more difficult to achieve. One word of warning here, though: there are a couple of limiting factors with this method which are worth remembering. Firstly, there is an optimum height before the fourth arm is overlong and the weight of the model, even if it is only a plastic kit, will cause it to bend and the plane to nose dive. Secondly, and again concerning the height, as the support wire becomes longer and longer the degree of 'whip' increases, shaking the aircraft rather alarmingly at the slightest touch.

For the 'heavier' and more rigid method, a length of wire cut from a wire coat-hanger is used. Again cut to suitable lengths the wire—only single this time, no tripod construction—is fixed into a base. This base should be as heavy as possible and ideally of metal, drilled to receive the wire-supporting rod which is fixed into place. A hole is drilled in the underside of the model to take the wire and thus the plane is supported. Once again, if several supports are constructed with varying lengths of wire, the model aircraft can be made to operate at different heights. The advantage of this method is that the 'whip' factor is eradicated, but it needs to be stressed that the base must be heavy and this may cause the wargamer to have production problems.

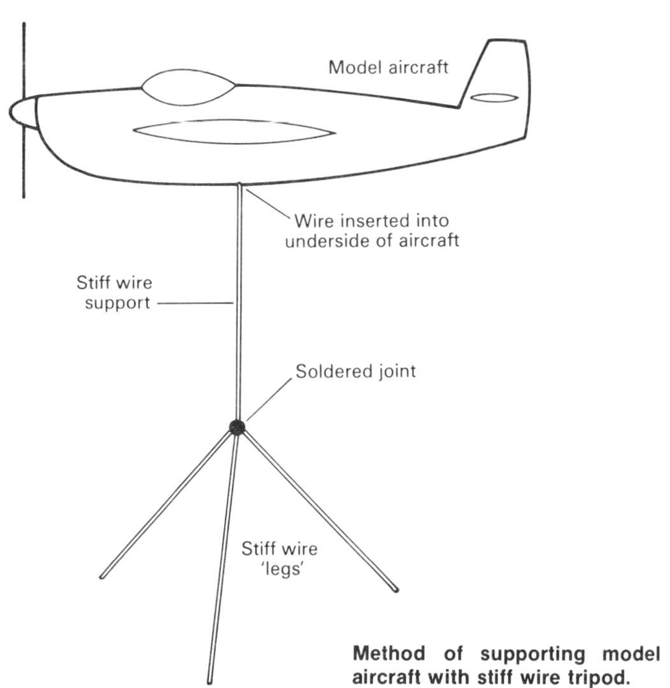

Method of supporting model aircraft with stiff wire tripod.

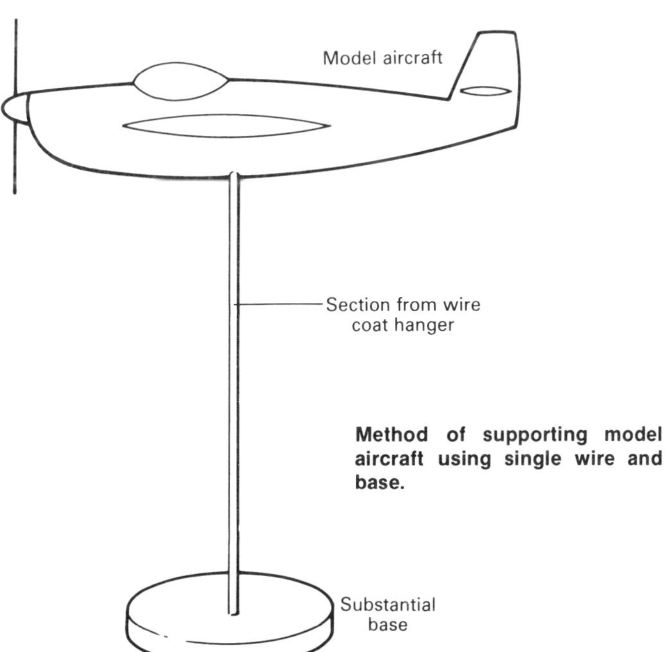

Method of supporting model aircraft using single wire and base.

In each of these cases, the actual length of wire which is cut depends very much on the wargamer and the scale of the models. While the first two methods can be utilised for air-to-air combat, those using stands are really designed for air-to-ground operations. It is fully appreciated that combat between aircraft was an important factor in the Second World War but, since the vast majority of wargamers only use their aircraft in the ground attack role, it is this mode of warfare that will be considered here.

There are three actions our model aircraft can perform: fly over the table, fire machine guns and/or cannons, and drop bombs.

Flying

As with other types of movement, the aeroplane needs to be allocated a scaled-down speed as it crosses the wargames table. It seems reasonable to stipulate as a base line that the combat speed of a plane operating in the ground attack role would be half its maximum speed. This gives the pilot time to line up the target and bring his aircraft on to a proper course for hitting same. The maximum speed of the tank-busting Hawker Typhoon was just over 400 mph, so this halved will obviously give us a figure of 200 mph. Now, it does not seem unreasonable to me that, given their relatively high speeds, aircraft stay for no more than one move over the wargames table. To ensure this, the 200 mph of the Typhoon is considered as enabling the aircraft to cover six actual feet. If a wargames table is longer than this, then the model can indeed mount two attacks—given suitable targets—in subsequent moves. The 'off table' time can be reckoned in the real distances and thus the number of moves before the aircraft reappears can be calculated.

Here's an example. Given a wargames table eight feet long, our plane comes in at one end, where for the sake of convenience, its initial move is deemed to start and covers six feet, and during this makes one attack. The plane then 'flies' two feet more, again carrying out an attack if required, and runs out of table. Thus, the plane banks left or right and, in doing so, is reckoned to cover *half* its linear distance. So, our example aircraft had four feet of its six feet move left and thus can bank left or right, a distance of two feet. Then it's a full six foot move in a straight line, a three foot bank and over the table during the subsequent move. Two points—firstly the plane will probably start its subsequent runs from varying distances off the table edge and, secondly, this method is, admittedly, wide open to cheating, but honour amongst players should prevail!

The 200 mph equals six feet measure can be applied pro rata to any aircraft—one with a combat speed (maximum speed halved remember) of 100 mph could cover three feet per move, whilst one

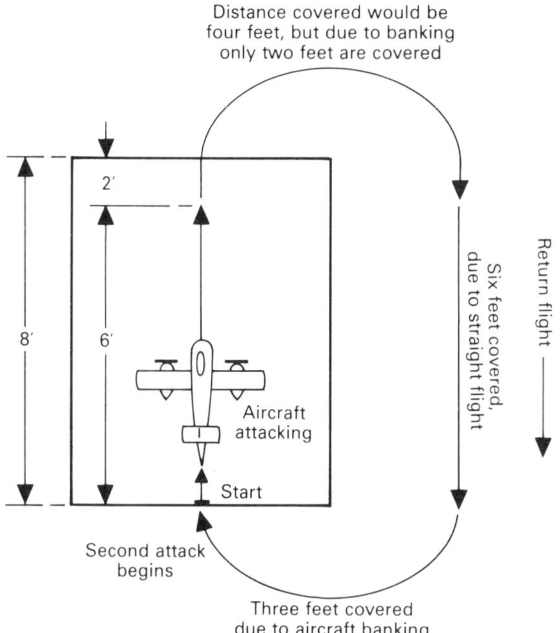

with 150 mph would move 4½ feet. Alternatively, if the wargamer wishes to simplify the rules, bands of speed could be drawn up, 0 to 100 mph and the plane covers four feet, 101 to 200 mm six feet, over 201 mm eight feet and so on. Such an action would have the built in advantage of preventing an aircraft from having a move of 3.86 feet or something equally horrendous!

Firing

Firing can take place at any point during the move of the aircraft, bearing in mind the range restrictions noted below, and is fairly simple to deal with. An aircraft cannon is given the same capabilities as the heavy machine gun was in the 'land' rules, while the aircraft's machine guns are assumed to be light in calibre. Thus, by reference to the rules covering the various aspects of heavy and medium machine gun fire, aircraft firing can be simulated in exactly the same manner as if it were land-based. It should perhaps be noted that if our model aircraft is 'flying' at above 500 mm it is out of machine gun range and above 600 mm, out of cannon range—a point to bear in mind when constructing support stands.

Bombing

Again taking place anywhere within the aircraft's move, the bomb is considered in much the same manner as one fired by a heavy mortar, with the exception of the 'ranging' mechanism. This is ignored, as a plane can bomb from any height, for a bomb falling to earth can hardly suffer from under ranging, but deviation and effect are still checked in accordance with the rules. The decision as to the number of bombs carried by a particular model aircraft can be left to the wargamer, but I suggest two per game as being a reasonable figure.

Anti-aircraft fire

It really is very difficult for an anti-aircraft gun to shoot down an aeroplane, and this is reflected in the rules. The firing procedure for the anti-aircraft gun in question is carried out in the normal way, dependent on the nature of that gun. Once a 'hit' has been achieved, two ordinary dice are rolled—only a double (any double) will indicate that the aircraft has indeed been shot down. Given that our model aircraft can typically cover six feet per move and the maximum permissible range of the heaviest gun is only 1,750 mm, there can be a problem deciding at what range the anti-aircraft gun actually fired. The best method is probably to utilise the artillery ranging mechanism appropriate to the calibre of the anti-aircraft gun in question, but in reverse by rolling a dice and letting the resultant score dictate the firing distance.

SCENARIOS

Air support requested...

The ground attack capability of aircraft can be incorporated into virtually any table top action. Granted, it is less likely within the context of a purely infantry v. infantry action, but even there air support could be called up by the beleaguered infantry.

In this particular scenario, the action is set in Normandy, a few days after Operation *Overlord*, the Allied invasion of north-west France in 1944. Pushing inland past Caen as part of the British 2nd Army's offensive in July—Operation *Goodwood*—a squadron of Sherman tanks from the Guards Armoured Division come into contact with elements of the 1st SS Panzer Division near the town of Cagny. Equipped with the fearsome Tiger tank, the German troops provide some determined opposition and halt the Guards' advance. The squadron commander calls up air support via regimental and brigade headquarters who promise assistance.

Whether or not the German forces have the benefit of any anti-aircraft artillery support is up to the wargamer but, to give the scenario an 'edge', they could perhaps be allocated a couple of Wirlbelwind tracked quadruple 20 mm cannon. The German forces can also have as many as six Tiger I tanks, with or without infantry support as requested. This dreaded tank was a real 'stopper' and,

Suggested Wargames layout for "air support requested" scenario.

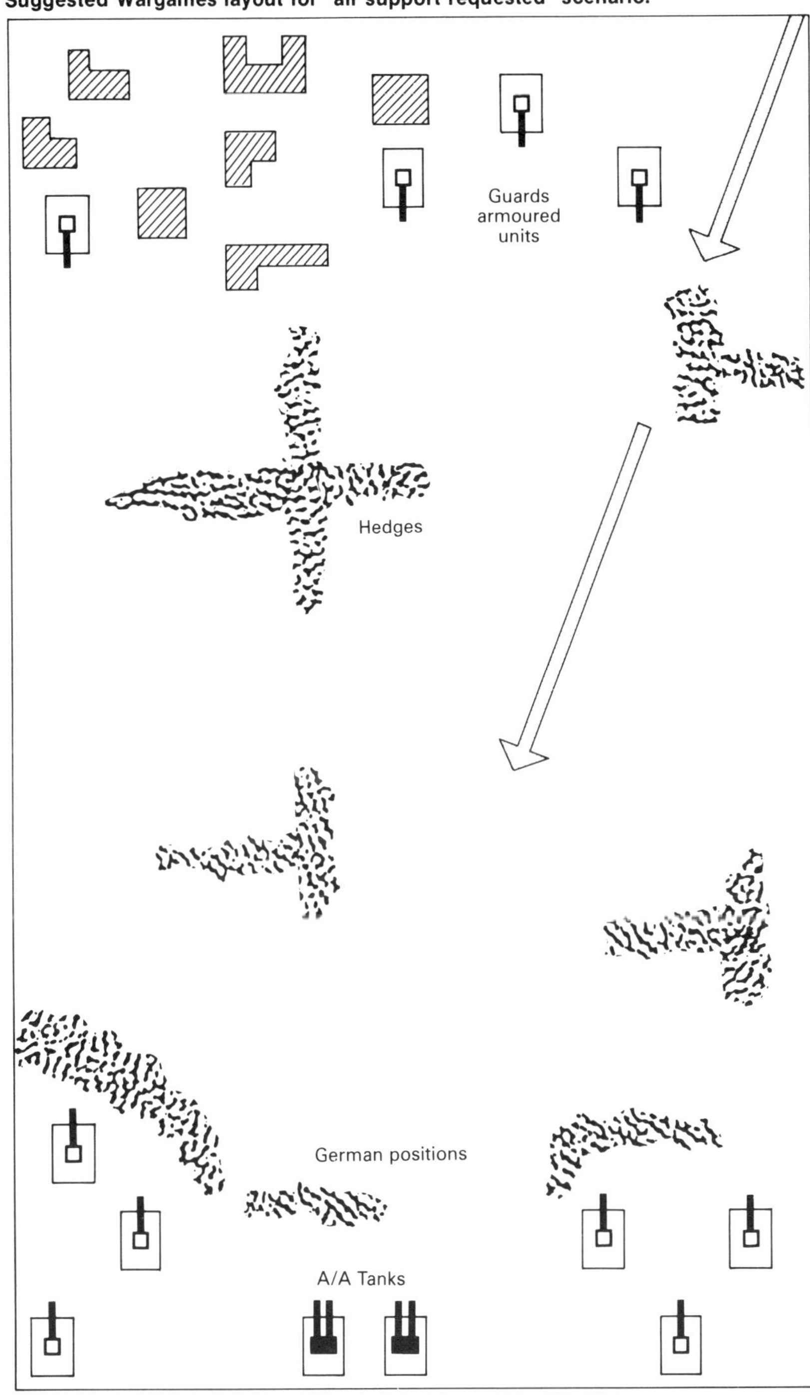

although they were few in number and suffered from an over-stressed engine, when its 8.8 cm gun was pointing straight at you ...

The Guards for their part can field either a squadron or a troop of Sherman tanks; much will depend on the scale of models in use in the wargame. Some infantry in half-tracks or lorries can accompany the Shermans, but they have no specific part to play in this scenario. The air support can be a flight of three Hawker Tempest, the successor to the Typhoon and even deadlier. Armed with typically four 20 mm cannon, two 1,000 lb bombs and eight 60 lb rockets the Tempest had a maximum speed of 435 mph, making it a very fast 'six footer' in our scenario.

The terrain can be either agricultural or urban or indeed a mixture of both, since fighting to the south-east of Caen took place in both settings.

The mechanisms for all the various weapons have been covered elsewhere, with the exception of the air-to-ground rockets. These can be classified as medium calibre anti-tank guns and treated as such in all respects. Wargamers may wish to reflect the possible inaccuracies caused by the free flight of the rockets once launched, but there should be a fair chance of them hitting their intended target. The rockets, being treated as medium anti-tank, have a maximum range of 800 mm which could be divided into sections each of 100 mm and one dice rolled for each 100 mm section that the rockets cover—this will depend on the range at which they were actually fired, of course. Anything but a six and the rocket will carry on along its intended flight path—a six and it will veer off and be lost. The aircraft can fire their eight rockets in pairs, all at once or any reasonable combination in between.

Gliding along on the breeze...

In addition to the somewhat glamorous paratroop formations, units of infantry could be ferried into action in gliders. Lacking engines, these were towed behind bombers and then released near their intended landing zones, guided there by their army pilots. The British army used three main types of glider, the Waco CG4/4A Hadrian which could carry 15 fully equipped soldiers, the much larger Airspeed AS51 Horsa which had a capacity of around 30 men and the GA49 Hamilcar which was a transport, rather than a troop, carrier.

This scenario is set as a small part of Operation *Market Garden*. the Allied assault on the bridges around Arnhem in September 1944. The 1st battalion of the Kings Own Scottish Borderers formed a part of the 1st Air Landing Brigade and landed to the north west of Arnhem itself.

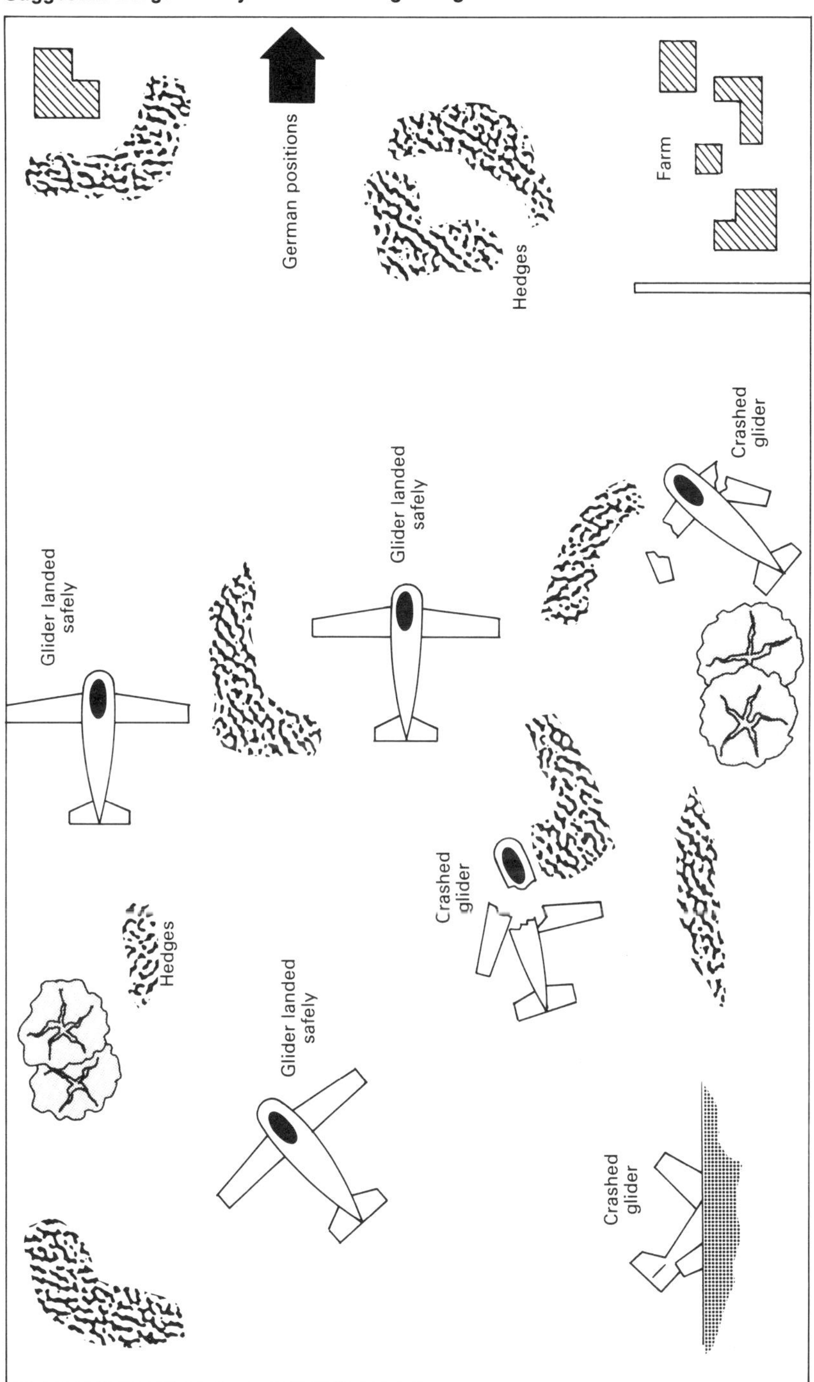

German positions
Hedges
Farm
Crashed glider
Glider landed safely
Glider landed safely
Hedges
Crashed glider
Glider landed safely
Crashed glider

The British forces can consist of a number of gliders commensurate with the wargamer's resources. Models of the gliders are available, but these are comparatively hard to find and expensive. Since only a symbolic representation is needed, a balsa wood knock-up will suffice quite adequately. Once the gliders are released they coast in, looking for a suitable landing site within the selected landing zone allocated to them. Here is the first wargames problem: will all the pilots find firstly the landing zone and, secondly, a suitable site? (Author's note—there is no inherent slur intended on the bravery, expertise and skill of the actual glider pilots by this, it is simply a mechanism to add spice to the scenario.) Let us assume that the wargamer has amassed six gliders. It seems reasonable that they will all find the landing zone, but any double on two ordinary dice means that they do not and are lost to this scenario. The next problem is to land the glider—using one dice, a score of 5 or 6 means that the glider crashes and its passengers have to be diced for with a 6 required for survival. Once the glider lands safely, the occupants disembark rapidly but can only move at half speed for the first move.

The main point of interest in the scenario is the landing of the Borderers for, once the gliders are down, the scenario takes on the nature of a normal infantry action. Some limited support elements can be landed with the British, for the Hamilcar could carry either a light Locust or Tetrach tank, or two carriers or two scout cars or a 25pdr gun with tractor and limber.

The Germans can shoot down the gliders with anti-aircraft artillery but, for the purposes of this scenario, the defending ground forces do not possess sufficiently heavy calibre weapons.

Kits and Models

There is currently a wealth of aircraft kits available, but production runs are frequently erratic—it's a case of if you see a kit you need, buy it! This will avoid trekking around model shops in search of that elusive kit—I swear that there were dozens on the shelf not a month ago—or worse, paying the ludicrously high prices demanded by the amateur entrepreneur for out-of-production kits. It doesn't matter then when the kit is assembled, it is there waiting for you when you wish to put it together.

Airfix
A good range of 1/72 aircraft kits which provides most of the popular types—at intervals. There are also limited ranges of less useful, in wargaming terms, 1/48, 1/32 and 1/24 scale kits.

Arii
A limited range of 1/48 scale plastic kits.

Ensign (Model Figures & Hobbies)
A range of 1/1200 white metal models

Fujimi
Plastic kits in 1/72 scale.

Hasegawa
Series of 1/32, 1/48 and 1/72 scale plastic kits.

Heller Humbrol
A small range of 1/72 scale plastic kits.

Italeri
Plastic kits in 1/48 and 1/72 scales.

Mainly Military (103, Walsall Road, Lichfield, Staffs.)
A small range of 1/300 scale white metal items.

Matchbox
Matchbox have a useful range of 1/72 scale plastic aircraft kits which feature most of the basic types and a smaller range in 1/32 scale.

Monogram

A range of 1/72 plastic kits, mainly bombers.

Nichimo

A smallish range of 1/48 scale plastic kits.

Revell

Revell produce plastic kits in a number of scales, 1/32, 1/48, 1/72, 1/100 and 1/144.

Skytrex

Skytrex produce two ranges of white metal aircraft, 1/200 and 1/300. In the 1/200 scale the main types of the war are all represented and the range complements the company's more extensive figure and vehicle range in the same scale. The range of the 1/300 scale series is also quite comprehensive.

Rules

Brocklebank N. *World War Two & Modern Aerial Warfare*. Active Service Press 1988.

Scott A. *Angels One-Five: Playable Air Combat Rules 1936–1945*. Athena Books 1988.

Books

Aircraft Archive. Fighters of World War 2 Vols. 1 & 2. Bombers of World War 2. All Argus Books 1988.

Asquith, S. *Guide to Wargaming*, Argus Books, 1987.

Asquith, S. *Guide to Solo Wargaming*, Argus Books 1988.

Barrymore Halpenny B. *Fight for the Sky*. PSL 1986.

Cooper A. *Bombers Over Berlin*. William Kimber 1985.

Featherstone D. *Air Wargames*. Stanley Paul 1966.

Gelb N. *Scramble: A Narrative History of the Battle of Britain* PAN 1986.

Green W. *Famous Bombers of the Second World War*. Macdonald & Jane's 1975.

Gunston B. *Aircraft of World War 2*. Octopus 1980.

Gunston B. *British Fighters of World War II*. Hamlyn/Aerospace 1982.

Lucas L. (ed) *Wings of War*. Hutchinson 1983.

Middlebrook M. & Everitt C. *The Bomber Command War Diaries*. Viking 1985.

Rickson P. & Holliday A. *Mission Accomplished*. William Kimber 1974.

Spick M. *Air Battles in Miniature* PSL 1978.

Terraine J. *The Right of the Line*. Hodder and Stoughton 1985.

Turner J. *British Aircraft of World War II*. Sidgwick & Jackson 1975..

Index

SUBSCRIBE NOW...

MILITARY MODELLING is the leading magazine in its field – for modellers, wargamers and military enthusiasts of all persuasions – which continuously breaks new ground and is a trendsetter within the hobbies for which it caters. Full colour illustrations provide modellers and wargamers with the information they need and give military uniform enthusaists and historians plenty of material to add to their collections.

PRACTICAL WARGAMER is published for wargamers of all ages and experiences. It covers everything from fantasy to hard-core Napoleonic wargaming. All periods and types are featured to produce a magazine wargamers have desired for many years.

Take out a subscription to MILITARY MODELLING or PRACTICAL WARGAMER and join thousands of other satisfied subscribers who enjoy the privilege of having their favourite specialist magazine delivered to their homes POST FREE*!

SUBSCRIPTION RATES

	U.K.	Europe	Middle East	Far East	Rest of World
Military Modelling *Published monthly*	£16.80	£23.60	£23.85	£26.45	£24.30
Practical Wargamer *Published quarterly*	£7.80	£9.90	£10.00	£10.70	£10.10

Airmail Rates on Request
* Overseas subscriptions include postage.

Your remittance with delivery details should be sent to:

The Subscriptions Manager (CG/18)
Argus Specialist Publications
1 Golden Square
LONDON W1R 3AB.

Here's 2 Good Reasons Why!